Black

Box

THE MEMOIR THAT SPARKED
JAPAN'S #METOO MOVEMENT

SHIORI ITO

TRANSLATED BY ALLISON MARKIN POWELL

THE FEMINIST PRESS
AT THE CITY UNIVERSITY OF NEW YORK
NEW YORK CITY

Published in 2021 by the Feminist Press
at the City University of New York
The Graduate Center
365 Fifth Avenue, Suite 5406
New York, NY 10016

feministpress.org

First Feminist Press edition 2021

Original Japanese edition published by Bungeishunju Ltd., Japan, in 2017. English translation rights for North America reserved by Feminist Press under the license granted by Shiori Ito, arranged with Bungeishunju Ltd., Japan, through Japan Uni Agency Inc., Japan.

The translator gratefully acknowledges the U.S. Department of Justice, Office of Justice Programs, National Institute of Justice, for allowing the reproduction, in part or in whole, of the sidebar "Learning from Victims," by Gail Abarbanel, which appeared in *NIJ Journal* Issue 243 with the article "Drug-Facilitated Rape: Looking for the Missing Pieces," by Nora Fitzgerald and K. Jack Riley. The opinions, findings, and conclusions or recommendations expressed are those of the speaker(s) and do not necessarily represent the official position or policies of the U.S. Department of Justice.

 This book was made possible thanks to a grant from New York State Council on the Arts with the support of Governor Andrew M. Cuomo and the New York State Legislature.

 This book is supported in part by an award from the National Endowment for the Arts.

First printing July 2021

Cover photograph by Tadayuki Minamoto
Cover design and text design by Drew Stevens

Library of Congress Cataloging-in-Publication Data is available for this title.

PRINTED IN THE UNITED STATES OF AMERICA

Praise for *Black Box: The Memoir That Sparked Japan's #MeToo Movement*

"These are not the words of a victim, but of a serious journalist. The vital urgency of Shiori Ito's record forces us to recognize the existence of the many similar cases that have gone unrecorded. Behind her words are the cries of countless others who did not speak up because of the intense pressure against them. I hope that these cries will not be silenced. I hope that someday we can progress further to a world where there are no such screams. This book is a step toward making such hopes not an impossible dream." —**SAYAKA MURATA**, author of *Convenience Store Woman*

"Such a beautifully written book, which means so much more when layered with the pain and injustice it covers. *Black Box* is Shiori Ito's story, but it's all of our realities." —**AMY RICHARDS**, coauthor of *Manifesta: Young Women, Feminism, and the Future*

"Shiori Ito gives a fascinating insight into Japanese social and legal mores, from 'quasi-rape' to the way women are treated in the media. Her account of her courageous fight against sexual violence rejects the harmful trope of the cardboard victim, reclaiming her identity as an adventurous, lively, determined, blithe spirit." —**SOHAILA ABDULALI**, author of *What We Talk About When We Talk About Rape*

"The crime of rape was rarely discussed and seldom prosecuted before Shiori Ito decided to charge her attacker. Ito's determination to seek justice, for herself and for other survivors of sexual violence, is admirable and inspiring." —**ANNE SUMMERS**, author of *Damned Whores and God's Police*

"Astonishingly courageous. Ito's determination to bring not simply justice for her own life but justice to survivors everywhere is a blueprint for systemic change. This is how you change the world. Shiori Ito is my hero." —**RACHEL LOUISE SNYDER**, author of *No Visible Bruises: What We Don't Know about Domestic Violence Can Kill Us*

"Ito's unshakeable commitment to demanding the world she deserves—the world we all deserve—shines from every page. Her story is a master class on how to refuse to be silenced, even when an entire government is set against you." —**JACLYN FRIEDMAN**, coeditor of *Yes Means Yes: Visions of Female Sexual Power and a World without Rape*

"*Black Box* is the courageous testimony of a young woman who risks everything to tell the truth about what happened to her. Relying on Ito's training as a journalist, the book is deeply researched and impeccably reported. With clarity and reflection, Ito's voice makes a vital addition to the chorus of those impacted by sexual assault who tell their stories in order to change the future to be a safer, better place for all." —**GRACE TALUSAN**, author of *The Body Papers*

"Shiori Ito radiates with passion and conviction for seeking the truth." —**RYUICHI SAKAMOTO**, musician and activist

"*Black Box* is a moving study of sexist Japan, political corruption, police failure to investigate rape, and justice sought and won by Ito's own efforts and investigation." —**JAKE ADELSTEIN**, author of *Tokyo Vice: An American Reporter on the Police Beat in Japan*

"While sexual harassment and sexual assault are unfortunately universal issues that are by no means unique to Japanese society, Ito's painful yet powerful account of being raped provides a unique and valuable exposition of the ways in which victims have often been deterred from coming forward." —**KUMIKO FUJIMURA-FANSELOW**, professor emerita, Toyo Eiwa University

*To all of the people who
have supported me to this day,
with gratitude*

INTRODUCTION

On May 29, 2017, I held a press conference at the Tokyo District Court. The purpose of the press conference was to publicize my appeal to the Committee for the Inquest of the Prosecution to reopen the investigation in the report I filed claiming to have been raped, which the Public Prosecutor's Office had decided to drop.

The incident in question had in fact occurred more than two years earlier.

The press conference was likely the first time many of those present learned of the assault. Yet, over the course of those two years, how many times had I repeated the same story—to the police, to lawyers, and to various members of the press?

At the time, an amendment to the criminal law concerning rape crimes had been proposed in the National Diet, as the Japanese parliament is called. The criminal code regarding rape crimes dated back to 1907, without any major revisions having been made over the past 110 years. This old-fashioned and outdated legal system stipulated that a person cannot be charged with a crime unless the victim files a formal complaint to prosecute. Deliberations about the amendment had been postponed, and I found myself wondering whether the Diet would ever actually pass the amendment.

There were numerous other reforms that needed to be made—not only this amendment to criminal law, but also how investigations were conducted with victims of sex crimes, not to mention society's general attitude toward them.

I needed to communicate all of this in my own words, with my own voice. If I waited for someone else to speak out, things would never change. I had finally begun to realize that myself.

This was the moment for me to come forward, with my own name and my own face on display, and for people at last to hear what I wanted to say.

On September 22, 2017, the Committee for the Inquest of the Prosecution announced its determination: "Nonprosecutable. Case dismissed."

Their conclusion sided with the prosecutor's decision.

But what "facts" did the committee base their decision on?

I had been told by the prosecutor in charge of my case that, because the assault occurred behind closed doors, the incident was a "black box."

In the days and months and years since then, as one of the parties involved and as a journalist, I have focused my efforts on how to shine light into this black box.

But each time I thought I'd pried open that box, I found yet another within the legal and investigative systems in Japan.

I hope by reading this book you will learn what happened that day—the facts that became clear through my own experience; the account of the other party, Noriyuki Yamaguchi; the investigation; and further research. I have no way of knowing what you will think about it all.

Nevertheless, if there is no possibility for this incident to be tried within the current legal system, then I believe it is for the benefit of the world we live in to reveal the details and circumstances of the attack, in the hope of fostering a broader discussion within our society. That is the main reason why I chose to publish this book in 2017.

When people hear the word "rape," many probably imagine a situation in which a woman is suddenly attacked by a stranger in a dark alley.

But in a survey conducted in 2014 by the Cabinet Office of the Japanese government, the percentage of cases in which a woman was forced to have sexual intercourse against her will with a total stranger was only 11.1 percent. The vast majority of cases involve victims who are acquainted with their assailant. Just 4.3 percent of all assault victims go to the police, and of that percentage, half were raped by a stranger, which makes it seem much more prevalent.

In circumstances where the victim is acquainted with their assailant, it proves difficult to report the incident to the police. And under Japan's current legislative system, if the victim was unconscious when the crime occurred, there are tremendous hurdles to prosecuting.

This was true in my case.

If you are taking the time to read my book, I wonder what you may already know about me. Do you think of me as the woman who was raped, the woman who had the courage to hold a press conference, or the woman who appeared on TV with her shirt not buttoned all the way up when she was discussing rape?

After the press conference, whenever I saw the "Shiori Ito" portrayed in the media, it felt as though I was watching someone I didn't know.

There were all kinds of things on the internet about this other, unfamiliar "Shiori" who looked just like me: she was a North Korean spy, a graduate of Osaka University, a dominatrix, politically motivated—these and all manner of unrelated and unheard-of details appeared alongside my picture. It was appalling the extent to which my family and friends—whom I had wanted to protect—were scrutinized. A month after the press conference, I heard from my friends that people were wondering where I was or saying that I had vanished.

But I was leading my life, the same way as before. I hadn't gone anywhere, and I hadn't disappeared.

Many things can happen in your lifetime: events you never imagined, stories like the ones you see on television, things you thought only happened to other people much different from yourself.

I aspired to become a journalist. I studied journalism and photography at an American university, and after returning to Japan in 2015, I began an internship at Reuters. And just then, something happened that changed my life forever.

I had traveled to over sixty different countries; I had interviewed Colombian guerrillas and reported on stories from the cocaine jungles of Peru. When people heard this, they always said, "You must really have been putting yourself at risk!"

But while I was covering stories in such remote areas of these countries, I never felt at risk. The place where I encountered real danger was in Asia, in my own famously "safe" country—Japan. And the events that transpired afterward were even more devastating. The hospital, the hotlines, the police—none of these institutions were there to save me.

I was astounded to realize this about the society I had been living in so blissfully unaware.

Sexual violence causes unwanted fear and pain for all its victims. Our trauma continues for a long time afterward.

Why was I raped? There is no definitive answer to this question. I have blamed myself, over and over. It's simply something that happened to me. And unfortunately, no one can change what happened.

I want to believe this experience isn't in vain. When it happened to me, I had never been in so much pain. At first, I had absolutely no idea how to deal with such an unimaginable event.

Now I know what needs to be done. And in order to

accomplish this, we must make changes—simultaneously—to the societal and legal systems that handle sexual violence. Above all, I hope to enable a society in which we can discuss trauma more openly. For the sake of myself, for my sister and the friends I love, for the children of the future, including my own, and for the many people whose names and faces I don't know.

Keeping my shame and anger to myself wouldn't have changed anything. That is why I decided to write this book—to speak my mind and to expose the problems that need to be addressed.

At the risk of repeating myself, I did not write this book because I wanted to tell the story about "what happened."

I want to raise questions such as "How can we prevent assault from happening?" and "When assault does happen to someone, how can they get the help they need?" The only reason I even bother to bring up the past is so that we can strive to have these discussions in the future.

There is something else I hope you will understand when you read this book: it is impossible to predict when or where what happened to me could happen to you or to someone you love.

In a 2017 amendment to Japan's criminal law, the crimes of "rape" and "quasi-rape" were renamed as "forced sexual intercourse" and "quasi-forced sexual intercourse," respectively. The major difference in these terms being that the old law considered only women as potential victims of the offense, based upon the former definition of rape as vaginal penetration by a penis; the revised definition recognized male victims by broadening the scope of "intercourse" to include forced anal and oral sex.

I will address the criminal law amendment later on, but for the purpose of this book I use the term "rape" that was in effect at the time of the incident and that is still generally applied to the crime.

Finally, this book includes descriptions of my own experience. Because it describes sexual violence, I hope that those who have concerns about flashbacks or PTSD will take adequate precautions for their own well-being.

CHAPTER ONE
MY LIFE, UP UNTIL THAT DAY

In September 2013, I was in New York. I had been studying journalism and photography at university. Between tuition and living expenses, I struggled to make ends meet. I had gone to the United States despite my parents' objections, and as a result, I received practically no financial assistance from them.

I worked part-time in a piano bar and picked up translation and babysitting gigs whenever I could. I was living with my partner, and working at the bar meant coming home late at night. As a result, he worried a lot, so I didn't take many shifts. But the hourly pay at the bar was much better than what I got babysitting.

Meeting Mr. Yamaguchi in New York

At the piano bar, I would often meet Japanese people who were visiting New York and hear about the various kinds of business they were in. My coworkers all had their own dreams too—it was a fun place to work.

That was how I first met Noriyuki Yamaguchi.

Whenever I made conversation with customers, I always opened with, "I'm studying journalism." That evening, when I mentioned this, a man drinking at the bar pointed at Mr. Yamaguchi and said, "That guy is the Washington bureau chief for TBS," referring to Tokyo Broadcasting System, a major media network.

Mr. Yamaguchi was friendly. "As a journalist myself, I'm always glad to meet people like you who dream of becoming one too." I leaped at this chance encounter with someone who had the job I had long been working toward, and a lively conversation followed. I was set to graduate the following year and had some internship experience, and I knew that I wanted to work on the news scene. It was thrilling to hear stories from a seasoned journalist.

Mr. Yamaguchi gave me his business card, saying, "If you have a chance, I'll show you around the New York bureau—please email me."

That was where the conversation ended that first evening.

Our next meeting occurred sooner than expected. Before the end of autumn, Mr. Yamaguchi contacted me on another visit to New York with the following invitation:

"I'm having lunch with the TBS New York bureau chief—want to join us?"

My classes had just ended for the semester. Excited, I arrived at the Japanese restaurant just as they were finishing their meal.

I introduced myself and ordered dessert along with them. After that, because Mr. Yamaguchi had business to attend to, he accompanied us back to the TBS New York office, where he said hello to the staff before leaving. Then, the bureau chief gave me a tour.

Shortly thereafter, it became difficult for me to continue my studies in New York. It was tough to juggle my part-time jobs, and the scholarship I received wasn't enough to cover all my school expenses. There were additional living costs, and as I started the year I expected to graduate, I had used up all of my savings. The cost of studying in New York would have covered tuition as well as living expenses at a university in Europe.

I had considered my course requirements and realized that I could study for six months at a university in Florence, Italy. I figured I would be able to get by there and still continue my studies. It wasn't easy to persuade my partner, but he reluctantly agreed.

As far as I was concerned, nothing was more important than my path to becoming a journalist. In elementary school I had written an essay about working on the news while doing research on animals in the savannah. It had long been my dream to work in a field that involved information gathering around the world. I had always been inspired by what I imagined other, unfamiliar worlds to be like.

Early Life

I was born in 1989—the year that the Berlin Wall fell, and the first year of the Heisei era in Japan. The first child of parents who grew up in the countryside, I lived with my family in a bedroom community in the suburbs. Despite having a strong sense of justice from an early age, I was a mischievous child, often driving boys to tears.

When I was three years old, I loved the anime series *Anpanman*. Apparently, I watched the same video so many times that my mother started to worry. I think it was Anpanman's influence that made me upset whenever I saw bullying—I even gave one boy a swift "Anpanman punch" and made his nose bleed. My mother had to bring a box of sweets when we made our apology.

I must have been quite the terror, if I do say so myself.

Not the kind of child who could be bribed with candy, I was stubborn and willful, unwilling to bend once my mind was made up. One time, I wanted my parents to buy me a dolphin-shaped pool float, and I threw such a tantrum, rolling on the floor crying, that they just left me behind in the store.

As a child, I always wanted to explore more and more unfamiliar places. I can remember being the lost child summoned over the loud speaker wherever we went—in department stores, when swimming at the beach, and so on—even though I never intended to get lost. Once I even strayed as far as the next town over, and the police took me into custody. I was four years old at the time.

Several years later, my parents got so worried that they almost called the police on me themselves.

This time, I had brought my friends along on my exploration because I wanted to show them the housing complex where we used to live. The place was quite a distance away—you wouldn't have thought that young children would be able to get that far on their own—but we actually made it there and then managed to follow the same way to get back home. It was pitch dark outside by the time we returned, and my friends' mothers were terribly worried. And it had been such a march that one of my friends had worn a hole through her sock—which only angered her mother even more.

I wonder how I would've turned out, had I been the child of overprotective parents. My pro-America mom was raised in the countryside surrounded by rice paddies and allowed me a surprising amount of latitude to roam free. At the housing complex where we lived until I was four, the fifth-floor balcony served as my jungle gym. I would often grab on to the balcony railing and hoist myself over, interloping on the balcony of my friend's apartment next door.

It's alarming to think back now on the hazards of how I used to play. If my own child were to behave the way I did, it would surely make me neurotic. I can only imagine that my mother must not have known about the kinds of things I was doing.

The New Role of Big Sister

Once I had younger siblings though, I took my new role of big sister—and my duty to protect them—very seriously. Before long, I had taken on babysitting other little kids in the neighborhood, and the area around my house had become something of a playground in the hours after elementary school.

My parents were very worried about my younger brother, who still hadn't uttered a word by the time he was about to start elementary school, and so they began taking him to see medical experts. A part of me was anxious that my overtalkative self had somehow robbed him of speech.

No longer an only child, at some point I had become aware that I was not under the same watchful gaze of my parents, and I went about doing whatever it was on my own and making decisions for myself—I was free to do whatever I liked. My grades were decent, so I don't remember being told to study. My parents saw my report card, figured I was doing fine, and kept their attention focused on my younger brother and sister.

My younger sister followed me wherever I went and always wanted to play with my friends and me. Even now, when I see my sister in dreams, oddly she often appears at this age. Perhaps because I left home so early, the memories of my sister from when she was young are the strongest.

Since we were so far apart in age, when I was in high school, we were frequently mistaken for mother and daughter. I always counted on her, my adorable little sister. She was the first person I saw, only hours after I was assaulted.

When my sister was just one year old, we were at the local public bath, and a woman who said she was the manager of a modeling agency came up to my mother and asked if she was interested in my sister being a model. The woman was very persuasive—"Just come in and see us"—and my mother must have been rather excited about the prospect. She agreed right then and there, and she took me along with my sister to the agency. I remember they even took photographs of us while we were there—"If you don't mind," she said.

But my mom was never really much of a stage mother, and since I was always up for going anywhere on my own and had no shyness around strangers, I was the one who ended up working. I was around nine years old at the time. They would send faxes, maps with instructions written underneath about where to change trains or buses, and I would head off to auditions or jobs.

When I was tired from working after school, I would stop in at my father's office in the city, and we'd travel home together. Honestly, the auditions—with all the children and their perfectly rehearsed introductions, glossy portfolios in hand—made me uncomfortable. It felt like I was offering myself up as goods for sale.

On the other hand, I enjoyed the jobs themselves. The process of working with grown-ups to create a finished product was interesting to me—had I not been a kid, I would have liked to be on the production side.

Once I entered middle school, my classmates started to notice that I was doing this kind of work, despite my attempts to be inconspicuous—I had only told my close friends, and I had used a stage name—and I didn't know what to do when the gossip started. At first it was just mild teasing, but before long it progressed to bullying. At school the norms dictated that "you mustn't stand out." As long as you were the same as everyone else, you were safe. If you stuck out, even the slightest bit, you were branded a weirdo. You weren't allowed to stray from the path laid out for you. This was my first taste of the pain of existing within the closed order of society.

The End of Being "On the Path"

I started playing basketball in middle school. One day I was on my way home after a game when I collapsed. This was the moment when my life veered off the path, the beginning of my hospitalization.

Time passed inexorably. A week turned into months.

My homeroom teacher came to visit me and said, "Think of how long your life will be—this is only a brief moment." And yet, I had the sense that I would be left behind for missing so much school—I was terrified by the feeling that my life had suddenly stopped while I was in the hospital.

When my teammates came to visit, I expected nothing to have changed, but I remember it seemed as if the air surrounding them belonged to a world that was now out of my reach.

Stranded on my own, even if I found my way back to the path, I no longer knew how or where to run to.

In order to make up for the studying I had missed, I started attending classes that were held in the hospital. This school was different than any other school I'd ever been to—we were even allowed to go to class in our pajamas. Not surprisingly, some of the kids were bedridden.

There was no pressure for time, and nobody worried about studying as hard as they could. Each student was battling a different illness, living out their own destiny. Not a single one of them paid even the slightest attention to stepping outside of any designated lines.

It was fun.

It was good just to be alive. Until that point, I had forgotten this simple fact.

Also not surprisingly, the friends I made in the hospital class came and went. Some were discharged, some departed from this world. It happened suddenly. There were a lot of goodbyes in that school.

I was discharged shortly before I was to start my third year of middle school. Once I returned to school, I realized just how small the world in which I had been living was.

My homeroom teacher did recommend that I repeat a year, but it was perfectly clear to me at the time that being behind in Japanese history or math lessons was not something that would affect my life in the long term. While my friends were busy preparing for entrance exams and deciding which high school they would go to, I spent my time teaching Japanese to foreigners who lived in the area and volunteering at a nursing home or a home for the disabled. I enjoyed doing things that were connected with the world outside of school. It made no difference to me which high school I went to.

After being discharged from the hospital, I dreamed of testing my abilities in a place where I didn't speak the language or know anyone. As long as I was healthy, I believed I could do anything. And I figured there was no need for me to return to the path.

When I told my parents that I wanted to go to a boarding school in England, they were vehemently opposed to the idea. On the one hand, they worried about my health—I *had* just gotten out of the hospital. On the other, the tuition was not the sort of thing that our very median household considered affordable.

I insisted that I would pay the costs with the money I had earned from modeling, but there was no way those savings would be enough to cover everything. Plus, my parents were now burdened with my medical bills and the experience of their daughter, who had always been the picture of health—hardly ever catching a cold, even—suddenly having been hospitalized. I had already put them through so much trouble.

Nevertheless, they also knew very well that it wasn't in my character to simply leave it at that. There had to be another way, and in my searching, a friend's suggestion led me to an exchange program in which I could live with an American host family.

With the amount that I had saved from working, this program was something I'd be able to afford. But it did not allow you to choose where you wanted to go. In my personal essay, I had written that I liked animals and nature, and so I was sent to Kansas. I didn't have the slightest idea where Kansas was, but even so, it gave me a huge thrill just to see the destination written in Western letters.

From Japan, I took connecting flights to Kansas, and for the final leg, I took a plane that only had one seat on either side of the aisle.

I thought we had arrived, and I was about to get off the plane when someone called out to me, "Not here, yours is the next stop." Like a bus, this small plane made several stops at various airfields, finally landing at an airstrip near the village where I was headed.

I was let off the plane at a deserted airfield, where I fought off drowsiness as I waited for whomever was supposed to meet me. You really couldn't call it an airport, and inside the building there was a sickly sweet scent—I didn't know if it was chewing gum or a cleaning product for the floor—but I still remember how relieved I was to see a smiling face over in the corner. This old woman was there to greet me.

The first family that welcomed me into their home lived in mobile housing. Their trailer stood on an empty lot. They were very kind and it was fun staying with them, but since they weren't well-off financially, it was a mystery to me why they had volunteered to host an exchange student.

Before long, though, whether it was from dust or something else, I developed allergic symptoms and an asthma-like condition, and I had to move to another home.

The new family lived on a ranch with more than three hundred head of cattle. The school bus would drop me off at the gate to their property, and it was a ten-minute walk to the front door. The surrounding area was so vast, and yet there was nothing at all as far as the eye could see. The landscape bore no resemblance to the America I had seen on television, but I couldn't deny the immensity of the land spread out before me.

I had imagined that my high school life would resemble what I had seen on the American shows that were popular in Japan—the teen drama *The O.C.* or the reality series *Laguna Beach*. Instead, this new lifestyle reflected quite a different picture: rather than the stories of love and friendship that played out in affluent California suburbs or beach towns, here in Kansas kids went to the rodeo on weekends or helped with the cattle drive. The first time I sat astride an out-of-control horse, it was all I could do to cling to the animal and try not to be thrown off. But after a few weeks, somewhere within me, a part of my body seemed to get the knack of riding.

In the beginning, I had no clue what was going on in my classes at school. I discovered that my classmates thought Japan was part of China, and their eyes popped wide with surprise when they heard that there were McDonald's in Japan.

At first everyone kept their distance—I was like an alien who had suddenly appeared and who didn't speak the language. At the time, the only way for me to communicate with my family was over the telephone—I had to use prepaid collect-calling cards I had brought with me from Japan. I was afraid that once these cards were used up I wouldn't be able to speak to them anymore, so I rarely ever called home.

I changed host families numerous times, and wherever I was, I felt the loneliness of being the foreigner, a lodger who did not pay for her room and board. But once I got involved in extracurricular activities, it was remarkably easy for me to open up with my teammates—that's the amazing thing about sports. My circle of friends grew wider.

After three months, I was starting to get the hang of my classes, even managing to keep my grades at the level where I wouldn't get sent back to Japan.

But the town was too closed off. There among my friends—who despite never having left the state still thought

America was number one—I felt a growing urge for connection with and information about the outside world, and I saw that this thirst could be quenched by international news programs.

During this time, the news I watched was an important source of information, my only connection with the world outside Kansas. I knew then I wanted to become a journalist. I was keenly aware of how vital it was to have this outside information. And I realized that it wasn't about merely taking in the information—it was crucial to understand it by doing my own research and asking my own questions.

"Leave a Blood Trail"

Even in a small town in Kansas, bad things still happened. An immigrant girl from Mexico was kidnapped and murdered. I still remember what my host mother taught me, when I first heard about this story.

"No matter if they threaten you with a gun, never get in the car with them. Even if they shoot you, run away. If you get in the car, that'll be the end. Nobody will ever find you. That's why you have to leave a blood trail. That way, there'll be clues to follow." This lesson was directed at her own daughters as well as to me.

In Kansas's wide open and desolate land, there were definitely times when I was frightened. If somebody hid me away in that vast space, no one would be able to find me. I'd never be seen again. That's the kind of fear I felt.

Fortunately, the year went by without any incidents that involved leaving my blood scattered amid the vastness of Kansas. When it was time for me to return home, we all cried and hugged each other goodbye. In my time as an exchange student, I had lived by the rules of strange and unfamiliar families, and despite the lack of various freedoms in an insular place where you couldn't go anywhere without a car, I had been given an entirely different kind of freedom— the acquisition of a new language. I now had the ability to communicate with more people than I ever would have imagined when living in Japan. There were so many more books I could now read. All of this gave me the confidence that I could live anywhere in the world.

My mother was surprised by the person who returned to Japan.

"What happened to my daughter?"

I looked completely different than before I had gone away.

In the US, having eaten my fill of all the food that was offered to me, I had gained almost twenty pounds. And before coming home I had visited a friend in Florida and gotten a deep tan.

When I went to say hello at the modeling agency, the staff was shocked by my appearance and ordered me to go on a diet. But I was in high school now and could get a part-time job on my own—I had no need for show business anymore.

Nonetheless, I would always be grateful for the fact that my work there had enabled me to study abroad at a foreign high school.

Determined to Study in New York

I set my sights on studying journalism in New York. I wanted to learn in a city where free-flowing information was its currency.

But tuition at American universities was insanely expensive. I thought I could try to cover my expenses with scholarships and student loans, so I requested the application forms, but my parents' income exceeded the requirements. It seemed unfair to me, since even if my parents' income was above a certain level, their support was not necessarily a given for my education. But I wasn't going to quit for financial reasons.

I worked around the clock at two part-time jobs. There wasn't time to sleep, much less see my friends. The only thing I cared about was saving up money, little by little, to bring me closer to my dream of going away to university.

Scrimping and saving all the time wasn't much fun, so I got another part-time job—this one at a TV station, working as a news assistant. They had been looking for candidates who were already students at a four-year university, but I applied anyway and aced the interview—I soon found myself racing around the news bureau I had yearned to be a part of, doing various tasks amid the constant buzz.

I never stopped—there wasn't a moment's rest—but instead of exhaustion I felt exhilaration and hope.

After almost a year of this, I made plans with a friend to visit someone we knew in Southeast Asia. I wanted to go to as many countries as I could, to see more of the world.

But I was so busy, there was no time to prepare for the trip. The day before I was meant to leave, I came home from work and started packing, but while I was folding clothes, I must have fallen asleep.

When I woke up, it was already the time when I was supposed to be meeting my friend at the airport. I raced there, without any luggage, but didn't make it in time for the flight's check-in. My friend had gotten to the airport and was already on the plane—just before takeoff, I finally got a desperate call from her.

I couldn't decide what to do. The price of a same-day ticket would have squandered the money I had worked so tirelessly for. There, in the airport, I did some searching around and managed to find a cheap, round-trip ticket with a return date one month later, so I grabbed it and set off to meet up with my friend.

For the first time, I had an epiphany about my situation. Any way I looked at it, I was at the peak of exhaustion—I couldn't ignore the fact that my plans to go abroad for university were financially unrealistic. At the rate I was going, I would work myself to death before I made it to New York.

After returning to Japan, the first thing I decided was that I would go to a university in Germany, where the tuition cost practically nothing. And so I left, but that didn't mean I had given up hope of ever studying journalism in the US.

I was sure I'd be able to find a way somehow, just as I always did. American universities charged tuition based upon the number of credits. I figured my strategy would be to acquire as many credits as I could at inexpensive universities in other countries, and then transfer those credits to the school in New York that I wanted to attend.

I wanted to begin studying Arabic in order to expand the range of topics I could cover as a journalist. At the time, there were a limited number of courses at the German university offered in English, and I had heard about a university in Spain that had a department in international studies with an exchange program in Syria, so I transferred to Spain. But that year conditions in Syria worsened, so ultimately I was never able to study there—though I was steadily earning credits, and I added Spanish to my course load.

I had been in a long-distance relationship all this time, and I began to think about how we might live together while we each pursued our careers and studies. I brought up the idea of moving to New York with him. He was excited about it and applied for a position in New York within his company. I myself received a scholarship. At long last, and after some detours, my dream of studying in New York was about to come true.

All My Efforts toward Becoming a Journalist

These detours had been stimulating. I had taken matters into my own hands, made plans, taken action—I had learned to find the means to realize my dreams myself. If I'd had the time, I would have strapped on a backpack and flown from country to country, taking photographs. In New York I decided I would major in photography—that's where I started making documentaries.

As I mentioned earlier, to solve my problems with school expenses, I had persuaded my partner to go to Italy. That was in 2013.

I returned to New York from Italy in the summer of 2014. Right before that, he and I had attended his younger sister's wedding, and just afterward, we broke up. I had finished my studies in Florence, and with graduation approaching, I wanted to talk about our future together. Unfortunately our views on what came next had grown too far apart.

His job would have him moving to a new country every two years, and he wanted me to go along with him—I could stay at home and teach yoga in my spare time, he said.

I liked yoga so much that I had traveled to India to study it, but he knew what my dreams were, and at first I thought he might have been joking with me. I couldn't accept my career trajectory ending like that.

Up until that point, all my efforts had been entirely focused on becoming a journalist. If I were to give up on my dreams—even to be with the person I loved—I wouldn't be making a decision that was true to myself. We talked it over again and again, and in the end, we decided to go our separate ways.

CHAPTER TWO
THAT DAY, PART OF ME DIED

I was back in New York in the summer of 2014, and with my graduation on the horizon, I had actively begun searching for an internship. I sent emails to people who worked in the media, saying that I was looking for work. Mr. Yamaguchi was one of the people I emailed. It had been a year since we had been in contact, but Mr. Yamaguchi replied: "There are currently no vacancies at TBS, but Nippon Television always seems to be recruiting people, and I know the New York bureau chief, so you might try contacting him." I checked their job listings online, and after going through the interview process and taking an exam, I began working as an intern at Nippon Television (NTV) in September.

The United Nations General Assembly meets in September, and reporters from all the bureaus gather in New York. The Japan-affiliated news agencies collaborate with each other—they rent a big conference room at a hotel and they all file their reports from the same location. That year, I was among those reporters, and Mr. Yamaguchi came to New York as well. When he realized that I was on site, he invited me to a meeting with several prominent people, including the Japanese ambassador to the UN. At the time, I was showing around a friend who had just arrived in New York and so I was unable to attend, but by the way Mr. Yamaguchi described it, I imagined it as a lively gathering.

In the end, I didn't actually cross paths with Mr. Yamaguchi that month. During my time in New York, I only saw him twice: when we met at the bar, and then when he introduced me to the TBS New York bureau chief. We never saw each other, just the two of us, alone.

As far as I was concerned, Mr. Yamaguchi was a successful journalist, someone who knew a lot of people and was friendly about making introductions. Nothing more, nothing less.

Working for Reuters Back in Japan

With the internship and my coursework, I was unable to work part time. I no longer lived in the apartment I'd shared with my ex and had found a new place with several roommates—and it was more expensive than ever to live on your own in New York.

Up until then, I had somehow managed to afford my student lifestyle, but now I had to ask my parents to wire me money. This also meant that my parents would know how financially strapped I was. Shocked, my parents demanded that I return to Japan immediately.

I had no choice. It wasn't possible for me to insist on staying. I promised myself that, once I was back in Japan, I would work tirelessly to find another way out.

The following year, in February 2015, I signed a contract to work as a full-time intern for the Japan branch of the news agency Reuters. I learned a lot from the work and from my colleagues there.

In the television news division at Reuters, news items were limited to three minutes. No matter how fascinating the material you discovered was, or how compelling a comment you were able to get, you had to be able to report on it in three minutes.

At the time, I was researching the phenomenon of elderly people dying alone. This was not strictly a problem related to Japan's aging society, it was a breakdown of communication, and there was so much I wanted to convey about the reality of people who leave this world having been cut off from human connection. I was simply baffled as to how to summarize it all in just three minutes. In the end, I managed to limit my report to a simple introduction about the location where someone had died alone.

I may have been better off working freelance, though I didn't come to this realization until much later on, toward the end of the internship. During my time there, I was also able to work as a stringer in Tokyo for Reuters's main Asia office in Singapore, and that's when I resolved to myself that I would carve out a career path doing the work I found satisfying. Having made up my mind to go full-time freelance, I returned to my hometown for the first time in a long while.

What was waiting for me there was my parents' strong opposition. My full-time efforts as an intern at Reuters were unpaid, so side jobs were essential, and I had taken on other work as a translator and interpreter. The stringer work had started to come in too, but it was still a struggle to make ends meet and I would need to continue taking on various gigs. I was working so much and barely sleeping, and my parents were worried about my health. Being bilingual, I had received several offers from foreign-affiliated companies for full-time employment unrelated to journalism—and my parents knew that I had turned these jobs down.

"Just work for a company for two years. Then if you want to go freelance, there will still be time."

I wavered in the face of such strong persuasion by my parents. I was their eldest daughter, yet until now they had essentially let me do as I pleased. I was a full-fledged adult, but I couldn't send money home to my parents—I couldn't even repay what I ended up borrowing during my time in New York. I felt guilty. And there was logic in what my parents advised. It's true that I had never considered working at a company that had nothing to do with journalism, which I'd been so focused on. Moreover, I was already behind in the general job-market search, and it was highly competitive everywhere.

How could I reassure my parents, and at the same time find a place to work that suited me, as quickly as possible? As I thought about this, I recalled a young woman who had found work as a locally hired employee with the New York bureau of NTV after graduating from an American university.

Perhaps there was a way for me, as a local hire?

The deadline was soon closing for when local employees of NTV would be hired. I had also heard that the New York bureau of TBS was not hiring at the time.

Then I remembered what Mr. Yamaguchi had said: "You can intern at TBS's Washington bureau anytime." If they would let me take one more internship, I thought, I could try to then parlay the opportunity into being hired directly by the bureau.

Résumé and Visa

I sent an email to Mr. Yamaguchi, six months after the last time we'd been in touch. This was on March 25, 2015.

Dear Mr. Yamaguchi,
It's been a long time. How are you?
Thank you for the introduction last year that led to my internship with Nippon Television.
It was an incredibly valuable experience during my last semester as a university student.
Currently I am working as an intern in the TV News division at Reuters.
My experience in New York was extremely helpful—I also received an offer to intern at CNN Tokyo.
Thank you very much again, I'm very grateful for your assistance.
You said before that I could intern at TBS's Washington bureau anytime—is it not too late to take you up on the offer? LOL
I'm in the process of job hunting right now, so if a local position were to become available, please let me know.
SIGNED, SHIORI [HEREAFTER, S.]

Mr. Yamaguchi replied quickly, later that same day.

Interns are soon hired as local employees.

Shiori-chan, if you have the determination to work as a producer (paid), I will take this under serious consideration. Please let me know!

SIGNED, YAMAGUCHI [HEREAFTER, Y.]

03-25-2015, 19:25 JAPAN STANDARD TIME

Working as a producer meant finding my own news stories and producing them through a specific framework while directing reporters and a camera crew. Having assumed I'd need to start out as an intern, the prospect of being hired as a producer was something I'd never even let myself hope for. I sent an email saying that I absolutely wanted to apply for the producer job, and Mr. Yamaguchi replied shortly after.

You do seem determined.

And so I am determined to consider your application.

Please send a PDF or fax of your résumé.

Also, do you have a visa?

A new position for a producer—regarding employment and compensation—will require approval from TBS International's main office. This may take quite a while.

Another option might be coming over here first and contracting as a freelancer, with an aim toward being formally hired while already working for us in the meantime. If you go about it this way, I can approve it.

Give it some thought and let me know which way you prefer.

Y. 03-25-2015, 22:17

I sent my résumé, and before long, two emails from Mr. Yamaguchi arrived.

> *I received your résumé, thanks.*
>   *The biggest hurdle is a visa. TBS may be able to sponsor you, I'll look into it.*
>   *By the way, I'll be back in Japan for a while on minor business—will you be in Tokyo next week?*
>   Y. 03-28-2015, 17:31

> *I looked into it, and the company seems to have a good track record of sponsoring bureau staff for employment.*
>   *Do you have any nights free at the end of next week?*
>   Y. 03-29-2015, 14:26

Ultimately, we planned to meet in Ebisu the following Friday at seven o'clock.

"There's an article I contributed to the issue of *Shukan Bunshun* that's on sale now, so read it before then," Mr. Yamaguchi wrote.

Friday, April 3

There are many different types of visas. Being a producer requires an official work visa.

Friday was April 3. That day, I was covering a ceremonial sumo tournament, and I set out for Yasukuni Shrine at eight o'clock in the morning.

I finished covering the story at 6:40 p.m., so I returned

to Reuters in Akasaka to drop off my equipment, and then headed to Ebisu.

The day's work had run long, and I arrived at the station an hour late. I had called Mr. Yamaguchi, and since it was too complicated to explain how to get to where he was, he came to the station to meet me. As we walked, I asked what had brought him back to Japan this time, and he said he'd tell me later.

But I don't recall him ever offering a proper explanation. He just talked about—at the bar that we went to—being back in Japan because his article had been published in that week's *Shukan Bunshun*.

Mr. Yamaguchi said, "I've already been drinking at the bar, but this isn't where we're going tonight—I made a reservation at a sushi restaurant, we'll go there next." He was born and raised in this neighborhood, so whenever he came home, he had to make an appearance at various places. "My old man brought me here for the first time. Do you mind just hanging out for a bit?" he said.

"Try not to eat much here," he told me, "since we'll end up at the sushi restaurant."

We entered a small, cozy kushiyaki bar owned by a friendly woman. Judging by his habits I'd observed previously and that evening's destination, I figured that he must have been there with one or two other colleagues from TBS. Also, from what he had said—"I've already been drinking"—I thought he had gotten a head start on eating and drinking with the others. But there was no one else there waiting for us, and in the back of my mind, I was surprised by the fact that it was just us two.

Although he had said we were just making an appearance, it wouldn't do not to order anything at all, so I ate the five or so skewers of kushiyaki that were set out before me. There was also motsu-nikomi stew and cucumber tataki, and I drank two glasses of beer and one or two glasses of wine. The glasses were small, and I've always had quite a high tolerance for alcohol, so I didn't feel drunk.

While we were there, Mr. Yamaguchi asked if I had an interest in politics, since that was what the Washington bureau covered. I answered honestly, "I'm interested in local news, though I'm sure I could try covering politics. What kind of work does being on the political desk entail?" He explained how, while on the local news desk you chased stories when they happened, the difference on the political desk was that it was all about building up your connections in that world. Not everyone was suited to it, but he said he thought I had the nose for both local news and politics. Since I seemed good with people, he suggested I could use that in politics.

Although I really didn't have much interest in politics, there would be much to learn in Washington, what with the US presidential election coming up the following year. I listened without taking it too seriously.

Mr. Yamaguchi had been busy chatting away with the customers sitting next to us at the kushiyaki bar and with the staff whom he seemed to know well, so it didn't seem like the right time to discuss my visa.

We spent about an hour and a half there, and around 9:40 p.m. we moved on to a sushi restaurant that was about a five-minute walk away. At the first place, my coat had been hanging in a spot somewhat out of the way from our seats, and because it was warm outside, I left it behind. But I realized it as soon as we started walking and went back to retrieve it.

I figured that at the next restaurant we'd get down to talking concretely about the visa and compensation. We sat at the counter at the back and ordered saké. We had a few small plates of food to go with two bottles of saké (slightly more than six ounces each), but for some reason not a single piece of sushi was served.

And the visa never came up as a topic of conversation. Mr. Yamaguchi did, however, mention the NTV bureau chief to whom he had introduced me, saying that he had heard very good things about me from him, which added to my perception that the evening was strictly some kind of professional appraisal.

The owner of the sushi restaurant seemed to know Mr. Yamaguchi fairly well; he told him he had read the *Shukan Bunshun* article.

Mr. Yamaguchi's byline had appeared in the April 2 issue, which had just gone on sale. The article was about public documents in the US that revealed the existence of comfort women supplied by the South Korean army in Vietnam. On the walk to the sushi restaurant, Mr. Yamaguchi had pointed out establishments along the street, "I went there recently with so-and-so," naming various well-known politicians, even a former prime minister. This behavior seemed designed specifically to create the impression of him as a journalist who moved within circles of power.

Before we had finished the second bottle of saké, I went to the bathroom. I came back to my seat, and I recall a third bottle being ordered, but I have no memory of whether or not I drank it. Then, suddenly, I had a kind of strange feeling, and I got up to go to the bathroom a second time. As soon as I was inside, I felt dizzy. I sat down on the toilet with the lid closed and rested my head on the tank. That's the last thing I remember.

I Woke Up in Severe Pain

The intense pain was what made me regain consciousness. I found myself on a bed, in a room with gauzy curtains drawn, and there was a heavy weight pressing down upon me.

I felt groggy, but without any of the sluggishness that you have from a hangover. Aware of a searing pain in my lower abdomen, and then the scene that leaped into my vision, I realized what was happening to me. I can't bear to remember the moment when I came to. Even in my state, in that moment when I had just awoken, with no memory of how I had ended up in that reality, it was unimaginable—impossible to accept—who the person was who could be doing this to me.

Looking toward the far window, I could see that the room was dimly lit; there was a light on beside the bed, and one on the console near the television. The light by the door may have been on as well.

A laptop computer had been left, oddly, on a shelf, open and powered on, and I could see the glow of the screen. The shelf did not seem like a place where you would place a computer to do work, and there was no chair set up in front of it either. Instinctively, something about the angle of the screen, pointing in this direction, gave the impression that it was recording something.

Neither the recognition that I had regained consciousness, nor my repeated pleas that I was in pain, made him stop what he was doing. Although my mind was racing with confusion about why on earth this could possibly be happening to me, the only thing I could concentrate on was that I had to escape. After my continued cries, he finally stopped and asked, "It hurts?"

And yet he made no move to pull himself away. I strained to move my body, but I was pinned down under his weight. Even when I tried desperately to push him off of me, I was no match for his strength.

I said, "I have to go to the bathroom," and Mr. Yamaguchi finally raised himself off of me. That was when I saw that he was not wearing a condom.

I ran into the bathroom and locked the door, my mind still racing with panic. The bathroom was clean, and there was a large mirror where I saw my reflection: I wasn't wearing anything, there were red marks all over my body and I was bleeding in some places. I remember seeing an amenity kit, with men's shaving supplies and such, laid out with horrible precision on a small white towel. That was when I realized I was in Mr. Yamaguchi's hotel room.

The Moment I Thought I Was Going to Die

I knew I had to get out of that room. With grim determination, I opened the door, but Mr. Yamaguchi was standing right there, and he took hold of my shoulders, dragging me back to the bed and throwing me down on it.

He held my body and my head against the bed with such force that I was unable to resist, and he started raping me again. When I shut my legs together and twisted my body around, Mr. Yamaguchi's face drew close like he was about to kiss me. Struggling desperately, I turned away, and my face was then pressed against the bed.

Pinned down and held this way, I couldn't breathe and, fearing I would suffocate, at that moment I thought to myself, *I'm going to die.* My parents would be devastated when my naked body was discovered in this state. Amid my terror, for a second I imagined my mother's crying face appearing on the morning news as they reported on my death. I knew there was no way I could let that happen.

I continued to struggle frantically, alternately stiffening or rounding my body and clamping my legs together. He finally stopped holding my face down, and I could breathe again.

"You're hurting me. Please stop."

Even as he said, "It hurts?" he was still trying to force my knees apart. I felt intense pain in my knees. We must have thrashed around like that for several minutes, my body stiff as I continued to struggle with everything I had.

Finally Mr. Yamaguchi stopped moving. I lay there, breathing feebly and looking backward, searching for the right words of abuse. Up until then, I had been repeating, "Please stop" in Japanese, but this was way too timid. I went straight to English:

"What the fuck are you doing?"

I could have said the equivalent in Japanese, but in English the effect is much more offensive.

"Why the fuck are you doing this to me?"

I went on, "I thought we would be working together but how can we now, after what you did to me?"

I only realized it later, but I had always used honorific language with Mr. Yamaguchi, assuming that he would one day be my boss. It makes sense—in Japanese, there is no register for a woman to use in protest that puts her on equal footing with a man who is her superior.

Before that moment, whenever I was abroad and someone would jokingly ask me to teach them curse words in Japanese, I had always felt a sense of pride in being able to reply, "We don't have words like that in Japanese."

"Let Me Keep Your Underwear as a Souvenir"

In a soothing voice, Mr. Yamaguchi said to me, "I've really fallen for you."

And then he said, "You passed. I want to bring you with me to Washington right away."

I could only respond in English. "So why would you do such a thing to someone who you would be working with? You didn't use a condom, so what happens if I get pregnant? What if you gave me a disease?"

"Sorry." Mr. Yamaguchi gave a one-word apology.

Then he said, "I have to leave for the airport in an hour or two. There's a big pharmacy there, so I can buy you the pills there. Let's take a shower together."

Those pills—the morning-after pill—weren't available in Japanese pharmacies without a prescription. Of course I had no intention of going there with him—my utmost priority was escaping this situation. "No thank you" was all I could muster in refusal.

After I finally broke myself free from the bed, my mind still blank with panic, I went around the room, picking up my clothing that was strewn about and holding it close. I couldn't find my underwear. I asked him to give it back, but Mr. Yamaguchi didn't move. I looked everywhere for my bra—it was on top of Mr. Yamaguchi's open suitcase. But my panties were nowhere to be found.

"Let me keep them as a souvenir," Mr. Yamaguchi said.

When I heard those words, my whole body went limp and I collapsed into a heap on the floor. I could barely hold myself upright, and I leaned against the other bed that was in front of me, hiding behind it.

It was a twin room, with two beds in it, and this second bed was still made—I distinctly remember that the bedcover was still on it, with no signs of having been used.

"Before you seemed like a strong, capable woman, but now you're like a troubled child," Mr. Yamaguchi said.

I needed to get out of that room as quickly as possible. He gave me my panties at last, and I hurriedly started getting dressed.

It was gradually growing light outside. I finally found

my blouse, but for some reason it was soaking wet. When I asked him why, Mr. Yamaguchi held out a T-shirt and said, "Wear this."

With nothing else to wear, I put it on without thinking.

I gathered the rest of my things and hastily left the room. It was only when I emerged in the lobby that I realized for the first time that this was the Sheraton Miyako Hotel Tokyo.

I had stayed in this same hotel several years earlier. The person I remembered being in those happy memories was so much different from the me who was here now. My mind was filled with shame and confusion.

Until I became a victim, I did not comprehend how violent sexual assault is.

Intellectually, I thought I had understood, but I had not realized what a devastating and destructive act it is.

Something had been brutally obliterated.

There I was, in the same clothes I had worn the day before, and to the naked eye, it probably didn't look like I had changed all that much.

And yet, I was certainly not the same person I was before.

It was all I could do to quickly cross that elegant lobby.

I didn't want to be seen by anyone. I felt completely disgusted with myself and, still unable to fully grasp the situation, I wanted only to get back to my own place, where I could protect myself.

I got into a taxi in front of the hotel. It was around 5:50 a.m. I wasn't sure how much time had passed between regaining consciousness and leaving the room, but I figured it might have been about thirty minutes.

Why had such a thing happened to me?

In the taxi, I desperately tried to remember the past evening, anything after being in the bathroom at the sushi restaurant and before waking up again, but there was a clean break in my memory followed by an utter blankness. Instead, what surfaced in my mind was the horrifying afterimage of being attacked, and a recollection of the accompanying pain.

When I got home to the apartment I was renting in Tokyo, the first thing I did was to take off all my clothes and hurl Mr. Yamaguchi's T-shirt into the garbage can. I put everything else into the washing machine and turned it on. I wanted to wash away every trace of what had happened that night.

I got into the shower, but I was bruised and bleeding, and my breasts were so tender that I couldn't bear it when the water hit my chest. I didn't dare to even look at my own body.

CHAPTER THREE
SHOCK AND CONFUSION

Even though I was back home and supposedly in a safe place, I couldn't relax or settle down at all. As I sat on the bed in my quiet apartment and tried to process what had happened, there were only flashbacks to the horrifying experience that had just occurred. I wanted to forget everything about it. I wanted to get away from the pain and the sensations that lingered in my body. I wished I could have flung off my own body.

A Phone Call, as If Nothing Had Happened

What the hell? I was confused by these unexpected actions from someone whom I had respected and trusted, and utterly bewildered since I had no memory of how or why I had gone to his hotel.

Just what had happened? I desperately sought an escape from the blank panic of my mind, where the same thoughts kept running through it. I had already told my parents that I would soon be working as a producer at TBS's Washington bureau—the only thing left was to figure out my visa situation. They would need to know what the latest developments were, but there was no way I could tell them about this.

Amid this absolute confusion, all I could do was curl up in the fetal position, there in my quiet apartment.

Around seven or eight in the morning, my cell phone rang. I answered it in a fluster—it was Mr. Yamaguchi. I had taken the call automatically, without looking to see who it was—although his number had not yet been programmed into my phone anyway. His tone was businesslike, no different from how he had sounded previously.

"There's a black pouch here—you didn't leave it behind, did you?"

"I took all of my things," I replied.

"I see, must be someone else's. I'll be in touch again about the visa."

As if nothing had happened, he had reverted to the same hierarchical pattern of speaking and, in spite of myself, I too responded in the same manner as our previous exchanges.

"Thank you, I appreciate it. Goodbye."

What could I have been thinking at that moment?

Mr. Yamaguchi was the chief of TBS's Washington bureau. Having moved within political circles for a long time, he evidently knew many powerful figures, not only among politicians but in the police force as well.

That wasn't all. At Reuters, the news agency where I had been working every day, their main business involved distributing information to various media companies. TBS was, of course, an important client, and their headquarters were located right next to Reuters's offices in Akasaka.

If I went to the police on my own and accused Mr. Yama-guchi, did I really have any reason to think that I'd be able to go on working in the same industry? TBS would act as his shield, and probably then sue me for defamation. If that happened, how would I be able to protect myself?

I was absolutely terrified.

By that point, the handful of glimpses I had caught of Japan's news scene had already made it clear that this was a man's world.

Maybe I was being naive. Maybe it was to be expected that I'd be trampled upon, kicked down like this, and I just needed to put up with it. Otherwise I'd never be able to keep doing this kind of job. These thoughts flitted through my mind, as if conjured by an evil spirit.

But if I were to have accepted these conditions, I would have lost myself entirely.

The pain I felt throughout my body made it impossible to ignore the fact that I was injured, both physically and emotionally. My mind was reeling, I couldn't calm down enough to organize a single train of thought.

That was when my younger sister called.

It was Saturday, and she had wanted me to take her to a café that was popular at the time. She was calling to say that she was on the train. I realized I couldn't let her see me this way—an empty shell of myself. It would cause her to worry too much. I made up my mind not to think about the attack, at least for today. Maybe, I thought to myself, if I could just stick to our plans and pretend as if nothing had happened, this whole thing might turn out to have been a terrible dream. I wished for that with everything I had.

When I think about that now, I realize that I couldn't have made it through that day any other way.

I thought I might go to the hospital before my sister arrived. I was worried about getting pregnant, and I wanted to get the morning-after pill.

It was still early, though, so I figured I should try to get some rest. But there was no chance that I'd be able to sleep.

I still found myself in a daze. Before I knew it, my sister showed up. She didn't know a thing, and although all I wanted to do was to stay in bed, I tried desperately to keep it together in front of her, not to let on that anything was wrong.

When I saw my little sister, innocent as ever, I was seized with fear, wondering what I would do if something like this ever happened to her. *Better that it was me,* I thought to myself.

I suggested to her that we go to a clothing boutique that was in the neighborhood, and then I ducked into the OB-GYN clinic that happened to be closest. It was a tidy office that specialized in premarital medical screenings. When I inquired with the receptionist, I was told that I could not see a doctor without an appointment.

I told her it was an emergency, begging that I just needed a prescription for the morning-after pill, and I managed to be shown into an examination room.

The doctor who came in to see me was a woman of about forty, with short hair.

"When did the failure happen?"

Her tone was brisk and matter of fact, and she never looked up from the computer screen as she typed up the prescription—she was utterly unapproachable. I felt help-less, which may very well have been a function of my state of mind. But if, at that moment, she had looked me in the eye and asked me what was the matter, I can't help but feel that the subsequent chain of events would have been totally different. Or maybe that's just wishful thinking.

The morning-after pill is taken in an emergency. All the more reason why that particular moment presents an oppor-tunity for identifying whether there has been abuse. What if there were a form to be filled out at the time when you obtain a prescription for the morning-after pill? The questions could be quite simple, yet this has the potential of helping many people. And if women's clinics were also equipped with rape kits, this would enable victims of sexual assault to be exam-ined and for the necessary evidence to be collected at an early enough stage.

No Window for an Exam or Advice

I should be grateful that I was even able to obtain the morning-after pill without a doctor's appointment. Consid-ering the tremendous physical and emotional damage I had sustained, the difficulty of locating an appropriate hospital on my own was insurmountable.

After that, thinking that I wanted another exam and advice about what to do, I searched on the web and found a nonprofit organization that offered support for victims of sexual assault. I called the number, and they asked if I could come in for an interview. When I said that I was hoping they could tell me which hospital to go to, and what kind of exam I needed, they told me they were unable to provide information unless it was in person.

Imagine how much it takes for an assault victim to muster the wherewithal just to make that phone call. In the state I was in at the time, I didn't have the energy or the fortitude to travel to wherever the help center was located.

In the meantime, the critical window of time in which necessary blood tests and DNA collection could be performed was swiftly closing. This was beyond my comprehension at the time, but part of me still laments, thinking I ought to have known this—somehow, on some level.

However, I still can't accept the fact that when a person contacts the help center over the phone, they aren't even able to offer simple coping advice. These educational sites created by public agencies, even the ones that appeared at the top of web searches, were they really helping anyone?

"Take it when you leave here," the doctor had told me in the exam room. I swallowed the morning-after pill, and then went with my sister to the fashionable Hawaiian café that she had wanted me to take her to. After that, I told her I was tired and asked if she minded going back to my place to rest. I don't know whether it was because my little sister was there next to me, or because of the pill I had taken, but I slept longer than I would have expected.

My sister just waited quietly, doing homework until I woke up. That evening, I had made plans to go to a hanami cherry blossom viewing party with a friend, so my sister came along with me. I truly did not feel like going out—I was in no state to go anywhere—but I was afraid that I might fall apart if I didn't adhere to everything on the schedule. If I stopped moving, thoughts of what had happened would rush in. That terrified me.

At this point in time, even though I knew I had been forced into having sex against my will, I didn't yet realize that it had been rape. As is common, there was a part of me that must have thought that rape meant being attacked by a stranger. I think that same part of me did not want to admit that I was now a victim of rape.

My sister had more studying to do, so I went out to meet my friend. Later my sister joined us, and we came back home a little before midnight.

My right knee was in so much pain, I could barely walk. The following day was Sunday, so I would have to wait until Monday to go to the hospital.

Dinner Out and a Painful Knee

On Sunday, I had plans to have dinner with my close friend K. and her family. Months earlier, she had begged me to be there with her. There was an important conversation she needed to have with her family, and the mood would be more relaxed if I were there, she had pleaded.

I was still not in any state to go out, but I hated to lie to K., and there was no way for me to tell her why I couldn't be there. I had received several calls and emails from her—at the time of the attack and right after—none of which I had managed to respond to.

Sunday afternoon, I finally told her, "Don't worry, I'll definitely be there for dinner."

Somehow I made it through the evening, and the meal was over. The restaurant was on the second floor, and my knee hurt so badly, I struggled to make it down the stairs.

K. had already been worried by how distracted I seemed, and now, seeing me on the stairs, she kindly suggested that I stay over at her parents', which wasn't far from the restaurant. She told me I should take the following day off from work, to have a doctor look at my knee.

I was afraid to be alone, so it was a relief to spend the night with her family. Left to my own thoughts, I would only be driven to anxieties—that I was pregnant, that I had an STI. Or I would obsess over whether I had been filmed on the computer.

It was then that I suddenly recalled something: date-rape drugs. When I was in New York, I had been told, "Never take your eyes off your drink." This was common knowledge, how to protect yourself against unwanted aggression. I never would have imagined that something so terrible could possibly happen in Japan, where I had thought I was so safe.

I searched the internet and found an American website that listed memory loss and nausea as symptoms that occur when a person has been given date-rape drugs—these were surprisingly consistent with what had happened to me.

Unable to contain my anxiety, I sent a text message over LINE to my childhood friend S., who was a nurse. "There's something I need to talk to you about." S. had just returned to Japan after living abroad and so, unsuspecting, she replied,

"Why don't you help me pick out some furniture?" So I ended up making plans to go shopping with her.

The next day, Monday, I went to a nearby orthopedist that K. had recommended. Even there, talking to the doctor, I could not bring myself to say that I had been raped by someone I knew. "I was in a strange posture at work. Must be because of an old basketball injury," I explained vaguely.

"You've sustained a severe impact, and your knee is dislocated. Surgery, if you opt for it, is a serious matter, and recovery takes a long time," the male doctor who examined me said.

He told me that the surgery may be necessary if the pain didn't go away. But the extent of the treatment I received that day was only electrotherapy.

I would spend the next several months wearing a knee brace. Even now, there are times when my knee still hurts, and whenever the pain returns, I recall the nightmare. My entire body goes cold—I'm struck with fear and a sense of powerlessness.

I returned to K.'s family's house and reported back about the doctor's visit. "They don't know what's wrong," I said. Even though I could talk to her about anything, she seemed so happy about how well dinner had gone the night before that I couldn't bring myself to tell her.

Then, I met up with my childhood friend S., the nurse. I described how my knee was hurting, and she brought me to a pharmacy and helped me pick out a knee brace.

We went to a café to have lunch, and she expressed concern that I seemed despondent, not like my usual self— she always listened so calmly to what I had to say.

"What's wrong? Did something happen?" she asked me over and over. But I couldn't find the words to describe what had happened.

"It's okay, take your time," she said.

And so I began to confide in her, telling her haltingly about the assault.

Her hand grasped mine so tightly that it turned pale and cold. And then she wept with me. It was the first time I had put my situation into words and spoken about it to anyone. It was the first time since it happened that I had shed any tears. For the past two days, I must have been in such a state of shock, the prospect of comprehending what had happened so horrible, that my emotions had been completely bottled up.

Later, I asked S. if she remembered what I had told her at the time. She recalled everything vividly. She said that I had been trembling, all the color had drained from my face, I had been sweating, and my hand had turned ice cold. She said that she herself could scarcely believe the reaction she saw me having before her eyes.

S. had been with me the first time I ever drank alcohol. My friend for many years, she knew better than anyone how high my tolerance was, and what I was like when we went out drinking or to parties. She insisted that it was impossible that I would have lost consciousness after only a few drinks and two or three bottles of saké. She also said that, knowing my character, it was unlikely, while out with a superior talking about work matters, that I would have drunk to the point of blacking out.

S. had also lived in New York at the same time I was

there. When I asked her whether date-rape drugs might have been involved, her reply was "Probably."

And then, with the utmost kindness and consideration, S. helped me figure out what to do next. Later, after I went to the police, knowing that I was afraid to be at my apartment where I lived alone, she was the one who accompanied me late at night to my parents' house.

However, S. did not have any better understanding of what to do in the aftermath of a rape. No one had ever taught us about that. To make matters worse, we were both apprehensive and unsure about whether the police or the judicial system would actually offer protection when the accusation was being made against someone with deep political connections.

And, S. said, even if there had been date-rape drugs, they were quickly eliminated from the body. "I rushed out of there because I wanted to get away as quickly as possible, but I should have called the police from the hotel," I said with regret. Still, the two of us agonized over whether or not I ought to go to the police now, unable to decide what was best.

A Journalist for Whose Sake?

I did not hear from Mr. Yamaguchi about the visa.

That night, I sent him an email. I wanted to forget everything, to imagine that it had all been a terrible nightmare. Parts of my body were still in pain, and my mind was still numb from confusion. Maybe as long as I acted as if this was normal, I could forget about it and everything would just go back to the way it was. To me, that seemed preferable to confronting and battling with the pain.

> *Have you returned safely to Washington?*
> *I would appreciate if you would let me know what you propose as the best way to proceed for a visa.*
>
> S. 04-06-2015, 23:01

But there was no reply. And anyway, I'd finally realized the fact that the producer job was unlikely to be decided so informally. I hated to think about it. Rather than having considered me as a potential colleague, had he just seen me as an "object" to do whatever he wanted with?

I was so mortified and sad, it was unbearable.

When I thought about it, there was no way for me to ignore or forget about what had happened. This mass that I had tried to hold in check—far from disappearing, it only loomed larger, continuing to torture me. I didn't have the energy to go to work, so I took time off, citing my knee injury as the reason. What pained me the most, though, was that in spite of my determination to become a journalist, to survive in the business of presenting the facts, here I was attempting to stifle the unforgettable truth within my own self.

For whose sake, to what end, was I so committed to this profession? If I was incapable of facing my own truth, how would I ever be qualified to do this kind of work?

It did not matter to me that I might not be able to work in the industry that I had set my sights upon. If I didn't live according to my principles, I would no longer have been true to myself, whatever work I was doing.

In the end, I decided to go to the police to consult them about my options.

Around this same time, I had made plans to go with K., whom I had had dinner with on Sunday, over to another friend's house, R. Both of them were worried about how out of it I seemed that night. When we went to the local convenience store to pick up a few things, I dropped the cup of harusame glass noodle soup I was carrying. Then, seeing how I couldn't manage even the simple task of adding hot water to the cup, R. stepped in to help.

At R.'s place, after listening to them talk about what was going on with them, I managed to get out the words, "I may have been the victim of quasi-rape." At the time, I had done my own research and wondered whether that term applied to what had happened to me. The crime of "quasi-rape" mainly referred to rape that occurred when a person was unconscious or incapacitated.

They were both extremely surprised, at first seemingly unable to comprehend what I meant, but when I described to them what had happened between Mr. Yamaguchi and me, they insisted, "You can't leave things this way."

Going to the Harajuku Police Department

My friend R. had been sexually harassed at work and had quit her job because of it. She had managed to wrest an apology from the person who had harassed her. However, despite having admitted to the offense in his apology, it was overturned in court. She knew very well just how difficult it would be, in my case, to get Mr. Yamaguchi to acknowledge any wrongdoing.

On R. and K.'s advice, I decided to resend my email to Mr. Yamaguchi. But since at the time it distressed me to even think about him, we decided that going forward R. and K. would help me draft my messages.

On the evening of April 9, I went to the Harajuku Police Department by myself. Five days had passed since the attack. I chose that police station because it was the closest to where I was living at the time.

I was in the depths of despair—I will never forget the panic I felt in my chest as I passed through the doors of the police station.

At the front desk, I had to explain what I was doing there, in front of all the other people waiting. I stated the situation in simple terms, and said, "I'd like to speak with a female officer, please." The person behind the counter kept asking me various questions. All I could say was "I was raped," but it still wasn't getting through to him. A bit more consideration would have been appreciated.

A woman officer took me into another room and listened to my story for about two hours. Then she said, "I'm going to get someone from Criminal Affairs." It wasn't until that moment I realized she was from the traffic department.

I had no desire to relay the details all over again—I was seized by fear, sobbing almost to the point of hyperventilating. I felt dizzy, like I couldn't get enough oxygen. I wanted to go home, but I couldn't leave.

I then spent over another two hours repeating the same story to a male investigator from Criminal Affairs. This may have been the first and second time I would describe the details of the attack to the police, but this was only the beginning. How many more times would I have to tell the same story?

After hearing what I had to say, the Harajuku investigator said, "You should file a report, and this will create a case file." Because of where the incident occurred, it fell within the jurisdiction of the Takanawa Police Department, he explained, and so I'd need to return when an investigator from Takanawa came to the police station in Harajuku.

By the time all this was over and I left the police station, it was ten o'clock at night. I was afraid to go to my apartment alone.

My friend S. had been worried about me, so she came and met me at the train station. After telling her everything that had transpired at the police station from start to finish, I decided to go home to my parents.

They knew nothing about what had happened yet, and I had no idea how I was going to face them.

"This Kind of Thing Happens All the Time, and There's No Easy Way"

But first, two days later, on April 11, I went back to the Harajuku Police Department. There I met Mr. A., the investigator from the Takanawa Police Department who would be handling my case. Once again, I explained the attack from the beginning. Mr. A.'s reaction was much more stern than that of the investigator from Harajuku.

"It's been a week. That's tough," he said abruptly. And then he continued, "This kind of thing happens all the time, and there's no easy way to investigate cases like these."

I had finally mustered the courage to go to the police, and it was extremely harsh to hear him say these words right out of the gate. The idea that this kind of incident "happens all the time" was chilling, and I was stunned that it could be treated so casually.

"It's very difficult to charge these incidents as a criminal offense. Without collecting semen or testing for DNA immediately after the fact, it's quite tough to prosecute without evidence," Mr. A. said to me.

"What about the hotel? They must have security camera footage you could check? Please get there before they erase the footage," I begged. Whenever I told any of my friends about this exchange, they felt angry and mistrustful of the police.

Now that I had gone to the police, I had to tell my family. The worst thing would be for them to hear about it from someone else. Although I was determined that it come from me, I had no idea how to break it to them. It was a tremendous challenge, but there were things I especially wanted to convey to my younger sister.

Specifically, if anything like this were to ever happen to her, she should contact me first, she should go to the police, there needed to be an examination with a rape kit, and after that, we would figure out what came next. These were the lessons I had learned for myself so far.

Hotlines and hospitals were not to be relied upon. I had

gone about it in completely the wrong way. It had taken me five days to go to the police. And even then, I had been slow to realize how much of a mistake that itself had been.

I thought of myself as the type of person who could speak relatively openly about most anything. But still, I had needed time to take this step. If my younger sister had an experience similar to mine at a hospital or with a hotline, she might give up looking for help.

When I finally got up the nerve to tell her, my sister listened quietly to my story. "If anything ever were to happen, I'm here for you, you can tell me anything, there's no need to worry," I said to her, and she nodded silently.

It pained me just to see my parents' reaction when I told them that same day. I gave them the simple facts of what happened, avoiding explicit details.

Still, my mother trembled with rage. "I'm going to kill the bastard," she said.

My father took his anger out on me. "Why aren't you more furious? Show some anger!"

I do hope you won't take my mother's words as a threat. Of course my mother knew very well that her committing a crime would only cause me more distress. And she knew that it would have been meaningless. I just want to convey her remarks and the emotional reaction she had, as my mother.

No Energy for Anger

The strange thing for me was that I simply couldn't summon any anger toward my assailant. Instead, my ire and frustration were directed at the police's response, and the hotline, and the hospital.

My father's words reminded me of something that one of the police officers had said: "It isn't convincing unless you cry more, or get angry. You've got to act more like a victim."

Later, when I visited a psychiatrist, I was told that children who have been abused will often speak about their trauma as if they are describing something that happened to someone they know. I could relate to that.

But whether or not that applied to me, I just couldn't muster the energy to be angry. There were too many other things to focus my attention on—cooperating with the investigation, and calmly and clearly reiterating the facts each time I described the attack.

I put all my effort into doing that. Had I laid bare my feelings every time I talked about it, it would have destroyed me, both physically and emotionally. At the time I needed every last bit of mental strength to get me through the investigation.

I continued to send emails to Mr. Yamaguchi. I didn't want to let on to him that I was speaking to the police. As I mentioned before, my friends R. and K. were helping me draft these messages, and their advice was to adopt as humble an attitude as possible, so as to elicit an apology from him.

And so, I decided the first thing to do was apologize for cursing at him when it happened, while still conveying my current state of confusion.

I sent the email and soon received a reply from Mr. Yamaguchi.

I don't recall you cursing at me.

I'm in the process of figuring out with TBS International in New York what the options are for hiring you. To bring you on as a producer from the start would mean increasing the number of staff at the branch, and we'd need to create a budget for that. If you were willing to come on as an intern, the hurdle would be lower.

As for a visa, since the producer job requires our sponsorship, you'd need to come here for an official interview. This would effectively be for form's sake—I'm sure you would be hired—but then you would need to return to Tokyo and have the US embassy affix the visa to your passport. In the case of an internship, an interview isn't necessary. I'm told this has to do with the different legal requirements in the US for salaried workers vs. nonsalaried workers.

Y. 04-14-2015, 19:18

Like before, he kept his tone businesslike and only discussed work matters. Disappointingly, there was no apology or acknowledgment of what had happened.

The Hotel Entrance Video

On April 15, I went to the Sheraton Miyako Hotel with Mr. A., the investigator. I didn't want to go anywhere near the place. It just so happened that there was no security camera in the hallway on the second floor where Mr. Yamaguchi's room had been, but they had identified the video from the hotel entrance. Though just how likely is it that, in a foreign-financed hotel, there wouldn't be a camera in the hallway outside guest rooms?

The video snippet showed Mr. Yamaguchi getting out of a taxi. Mr. Yamaguchi stood there for a while, and eventually he leaned his upper body into the back seat and dragged me out. Then he propped me up to carry me, since I couldn't walk on my own, as the hotel bellman stood there watching.

It gave me goose bumps to see myself like that, having no memory of it at all. It made me nauseous. It was terrifying.

Seeing the video, Mr. A. seemed to acknowledge for the first time that I might have a case. And yet, he still had this to say: "This guy is famous and in a position of power, and you work in the same industry as him, don't you? From now on, most likely, you won't be able to keep working in that business. All the hard work that you've done up until now will go to waste."

Mr. A. repeated himself, expressing concern about my future, telling me to reconsider filing a report.

After that, it would be necessary to confirm the video and view it once more at the Takanawa Police Department. I was scared to see it again, so I asked my friend K. to come with me. They told me repeatedly that she couldn't come into the interrogation room with me, but I insisted that she wouldn't say a word, and finally they allowed her to accompany me. K. shuddered when she saw my limp body being carried— she'd never seen anything like it before. Later she said she too was nauseated by it.

After the footage at the entrance, we saw the video of us traversing the lobby. As I was being carried by Mr. Yamaguchi, my feet didn't touch the ground, and I slumped forward as I was helplessly dragged toward the elevators before disappearing.

The final clip showed me scurrying through the lobby, my face downcast as I fled the hotel.

We could try DNA testing, Mr. A. said to me, but I had already washed everything I had been wearing. Regardless, I gathered the items I had worn that night, but for some reason the only thing I couldn't find was my bra. I tried looking for it, and finally found it—when I had undressed, I had put everything on a shelf and it must have slipped down to the side of it. Finding one article of unlaundered clothing gave me hope.

I had not yet responded to Mr. Yamaguchi's reply from the other day, and two days later, another message from him arrived.

> *Did you receive my email? Did you read it?*
>
> *In our industry, it's very important to respond to business-related messages promptly and properly. Shiori-chan, I'm working on all sorts of ideas about ways to hire you. Then when I don't hear back from you, I wonder if you've lost your enthusiasm. If that's the case, the polite thing to do would be to tell me so.*
>
> Y. 04-16-2015, 11:13

I had refrained from responding to him while hoping for further developments with the police, and in the meantime, another email arrived.

> *There's been some progress with your employment. Please respond just to let me know whether you are still interested.*
>
> Y. 04-17-2015, 2:00

I couldn't leave things any longer without raising his suspicions. I responded, making up a reason why I hadn't been in touch.

I've been in the hospital for the past few days so I was unable to respond. What kind of progress do you mean?

S. 04-17-2015, 19:50

I had not actually been in the hospital, but that day, I had made an hour-and-a-half trip from my house to Edogawa-ku, to visit a gynecology clinic with a supposedly positive approach to treating victims of sexual assault. I had expected that since the clinic's emphasis was on the damage from sexual violence, I might be treated appropriately, and so I had gone to the trouble of making an appointment and getting myself there. My hopes were disappointed.

I had been shown into a small room, where a nurse had stared at a calendar and robotically repeated questions to me. It was as if I were being interrogated.

After answering perfunctorily, I sat back in the chair that automatically spreads your legs when you're in it. The seat was raised, and the doctor examined me. Within a short period of time, I showed my most intimate area to these strangers. It was humiliating, but this was an exam that needed to be performed.

After it was finished, the doctor said to me, "The good thing is, there are no major injuries. There's no damage." He also said that too much time had elapsed since the incident. Apparently, this area of the body heals quickly. I understood what the gynecologist's diagnosis meant, that there was no damage, but the words were utterly inconsistent with the way that I actually felt.

And then, as if checking items off a list, he asked, "Are you able to sleep?"

I was given a prescription for sleeping pills, told that the test results would be available in a few days, and sent home.

"Did I Use My Authority to Hit On You or Make Advances?"

Mr. Yamaguchi's reply arrived.

> *You were in the hospital—are you okay?*
> *Here's the progress: in the lead-up to the presidential election, it looks as though the branch will be allowed to add a staff position. What kind of person will be hired is now under consideration.*
>
> Y. 04-17-2015, 20:49

Once my criminal complaint was filed, the investigation would begin. The hope was to force Mr. Yamaguchi to acknowledge the facts over email before the police spoke with him. Up until that point, Mr. Yamaguchi had written only about work matters in his messages. Also, we didn't know when the police would be able to question him, since he was abroad. As time went by, he might claim not to remember.

And when the investigation began, would Mr. Yamaguchi tell the truth? Whether or not he would acknowledge the rape over email, I at least wanted an apology. I conferred with my friends and composed the following message.

The last time you were back in Japan, I accepted your invitation to meet to discuss lingering questions about a work visa, regarding my hope of employment—either as a new producer or on a freelance basis.

Nevertheless, after bringing me to your hotel while I was in an unconscious state and engaging in unprotected sexual activity, why did you call me on the phone about the visa process as if nothing had happened? And why do you persist, even now, in maintaining these dubious responses?

Considering these circumstances, it would seem to me that you may have seen an opportunity for something like this to happen, under the pretext of a business conversation.

I had already told my family about you as well as about this job prospect, so whenever they ask about the progress of my employment, I am pained to know how to respond to them. . . .

If you mean what you have said so far, please demonstrate your sincerity. I expressed my own shock in a previous email and wondered why you did not apologize. In addition, I ask you to cover my medical expenses.

S. 04-18-2015, 20:36

About one hour later, his reply arrived.

I did not know you saw things that way.

I wasn't the one who forced you to do anything, you drank so much that you were in a stupor—you vomited in

the taxi, on my suit, on my briefcase, and lost consciousness.
I couldn't just leave you on the street, so I had no choice but
to bring you to where I was staying. You vomited in my hotel
room and in the bathroom, and I'm the one who cleaned all
that up. There was vomit on some of my important official
documents, and it cost time and money to have those reissued.

If you had eaten and drank normally, and then gone
home normally, none of this would have happened. From
the start, I would never have such intentions with someone
I expected to work with as a colleague. Did I ever once use
my authority to hit on you or make advances? Never! It's a
shame that you reduce yourself to the victim and me to the
perpetrator, and that you think I was so malicious all along.

And what do you mean by "dubious responses"? I think
highly of your passion and enthusiasm, and I continue to do
things for you. It's very complicated at this time to increase
staff in a foreign branch office.

If there are expenses related to what happened that night,
I think I can take care of those. But please reflect upon your
own behavior. If you can handle a calm discussion, please
email me again.

Y. 04-18-2015, 21:50

I had no memory of drinking myself into a stupor. But here
is what I thought was the most important thing in his email:
Did I ever once use my authority to hit on you or make advances?
Never!

More than anything, I hated the idea that someone could
have suspected I had gone with him to his hotel as a means
to gain a work favor from his influence. He had in fact introduced me to people, and I had used him as a reference, but

when I first met Mr. Yamaguchi, that had never been my intention.

It was an important fact that Mr. Yamaguchi had acknowledged himself. But here, now, I requested another more specific apology.

I am sending this email because I want to talk this through calmly.

If you took care of me, as you say, I thank you for that.

However, you engaged in unprotected sexual activity with me while I was unconscious, and since then I have been consumed with worry about what to do if I am pregnant.

Have you considered that possibility?

I had been thinking that I would be devoting myself to my career, and now I am terrified at the prospect of not being able to work because of a pregnancy.

S. 04-18-2015, 22:44

These were my honest and true feelings. Although I had obtained a prescription for the morning-after pill only hours after the attack, it was well past the date when I expected my menstrual cycle to begin. The pill was not 100 percent effective in preventing pregnancy.

His response arrived about an hour later.

That night, once we were in my room, you vomited in two places and then ran into the bathroom. I scraped the vomit in my suitcase and on my computer into a bag, wiped them clean with a damp towel, and then I found you in the bathroom, passed out on the floor in a pool of vomit. I peeled you up off the floor and removed your vomit-covered blouse and slacks, brought you back into the room and lay you down on the bed. I then went back into the bathroom where I used the shower nozzle to wash away the vomit spewed about. However, there was so much vomit on your blouse, and I knew you would need something to wear the next morning, so I rinsed it off and hung it to dry on a hanger. Then when I went back into the room, you were already asleep, snoring. I couldn't bear the stink of the puke in your hair so I slept on the other bed.

Afterward, you got up suddenly and went into the bathroom, and when you came back you got into bed with me. At that time, you said something like, "I drank too much," and you were speaking normally. So to say that I had my way with you while you were unconscious is completely untrue. I was also quite drunk, and when a beautiful woman like you got into bed with me half-naked, things happened. I think we both need to reflect on that, but for you to accuse me by saying it was one-sided, I absolutely won't accept that.

There's no possible way you're pregnant. But I do understand that it would make you anxious, and I will be glad to do whatever I can to help. But, in order to deal with your problems, you need to stop thinking of yourself as the only victim here.

Y. 04-18-2015, 23:51

Here were revealed some of the details from that night. He had described the timeline, of which I had no memory. Since Mr. Yamaguchi was in the US and wouldn't be able to sit for questioning, I had felt it was important to ask him about this over email, before his memory faded—and now he wouldn't be able to change his story.

He wrote, *I couldn't bear the stink of the puke in your hair so I slept on the other bed*, but I clearly remembered that the other bed was still made—the bed covering was completely intact.

My friend R., who had left her job because of sexual harassment, had told me about the Japan Legal Support Center, which offered free legal advice, so I decided to go there.

On April 23, I met with a lawyer. Once again, I explained what had happened from the start. I also showed the lawyer the emails that had been exchanged up until that point.

In that first consultation, the lawyer explained certain things, which enabled me to clarify several problematic issues.

In the case of quasi-rape, there are two issues that require proof: Did sexual intercourse occur? Was it consensual?

In order to prove that it was not consensual, the hotel's security camera footage would be essential. The lawyer advised me that it would be a good idea to obtain a copy of the video, for what would come next.

However, the police would not allow me to use their copy of the video, even though I was the victim—the lawyer said I would need to get it directly from the hotel. I had no idea how to go about getting them to give it to me.

Had I not filed a criminal complaint, the police would not have been obligated to keep the video. I was consumed with anxiety, to think how easily the most important piece of evidence, the item that would prove the act was not consensual, could have slipped away.

In the meantime, I had no choice but to wait while my complaint was quickly drawn up. I also wanted the lawyer to accompany me to the hotel to get the video directly from them, but he couldn't guarantee he'd be able to do that. This was free legal advice, after all, so it was unlikely he could do more.

The lawyer advised me that, while the email exchange would be helpful, it made no explicit reference to what had transpired.

On April 24, I sent another email, focused on one particular point.

I still haven't gotten my period—I can't help but be anxious, it's all I think about night and day. Why would you say that there's no possible way I could be pregnant? Please explain yourself.

S. 04-24-2015, 11:48

"Can You Give the Exact Time?"

Mr. Yamaguchi's reply was not forthcoming.

On April 27, I heard from Mr. A., the investigator in charge of my case. While he had been somewhat positive after seeing the hotel security camera footage, now his attitude was completely different.

"We can't arrest him. It's challenging without any evidence," he said categorically.

By evidence, I assumed he meant DNA. That being the case, I asked about the prospect of requesting a DNA test on my bra that I had found.

"Like I told you, even if it showed up, it would only prove that he touched you, not that there was sexual activity. There isn't even any semen. It's very tough to convict someone. The rule is innocent until proven guilty," he said forcefully. And since the questioning would be voluntary, Mr. A. continued, if Mr. Yamaguchi doesn't come back from Washington, the case stalls. And we can't go to Washington ourselves, he said.

Shortly before that, there had been an article published in the *Fuji Evening Edition* of *Sankei Shimbun*, which said that Mr. Yamaguchi had been demoted to a sales position in Tokyo. I heard from a friend that Mr. Yamaguchi had posted on Facebook a photograph of a news kiosk displaying issues of *Fuji Evening Edition* that featured this article. It was out of the ordinary for an article to be written about a journalist's transfer, and even more extraordinary that it would be about a Washington bureau chief's reassignment to sales.

Mr. A. asked when this demotion would happen, and after I replied that I didn't know, Mr. A. suggested we shouldn't dwell on uncertain details.

"What about the fact that he probably filmed me on his computer, can't you arrest him for that?" I asked.

His response was again forceful. "We can't arrest someone based on suspicion alone—it helps if there's evidence, but you don't even remember what happened."

While I was surprised by his vehemence, I countered that my memories were quite clear after I regained consciousness.

"Can you give the exact time when you woke up?" he said.

Calculating backward from the time I had left the hotel, I was sure that it had been sometime after five in the morning, but I had been so desperate to escape that I couldn't identify with confidence the exact time I regained consciousness.

"Your memory can't be vague—it won't hold up in court unless you're 100 percent sure," he retorted sharply. "And how will you prove it to the defense? In court they'll ask why you don't know anything more. They'll say it's strange that you have no memory but then suddenly it comes back."

I was frustrated.

Why didn't I have any memory of that night? Why had I suddenly awakened? These were questions I myself wanted answers to. My own uncertainty about these issues is what made me hesitate in swiftly filing charges.

At last, Mr. A. said, "But if you still want to file a criminal complaint, I will process it."

Why couldn't he be more encouraging, even just about taking my complaint? I felt a wave of despair as I hung up the phone.

With Mr. Yamaguchi's Demotion, "There Might Still Be a Chance"

The following day, there was another sudden development. Mr. A. called me in the morning. "There might still be a chance," he said. Mr. A. had looked into it, and Mr. Yamaguchi's demotion was in fact true—he was on a fifteen-day suspension, and apparently in Japan at the time, so Mr. A. was hoping to bring him in right away for voluntary questioning. He wanted me to file the criminal complaint immediately.

Even though the day before he had seemed so disinterested in me doing just that.

I was surprised by this urgency, but the next day was a national holiday, so if I didn't do it today, Mr. A. would lose yet another day, he told me, and he couldn't make a move without the criminal complaint.

But the shift in Mr. A.'s attitude and now hearing him say that there might still be a chance gave me pause. And besides, there was a pretty big difference between arresting Mr. Yamaguchi and bringing him in for voluntary questioning.

I remained skeptical, and I persisted in asking for more information. I then learned what had been happening internally with the police.

Mr. A. had given a preliminary report to the public prosecutor letting him know that I was going to file a formal criminal complaint, and it seemed the prosecutor's response had been rather negative.

Mr. A. summarized their conversation:

In a criminal case, it's the public prosecutor who is really the one in control. The police report on the investigation to the prosecutor, and the prosecutor reviews it and gives instructions about gathering evidence. If there's nothing further to investigate, then the police gather the documents and send them to the Public Prosecutors Office. This is all part of the process. And finally, the one who decides whether or not to indict on charges is the public prosecutor.

Mr. A. had consulted with the public prosecutor, who had told him abruptly, "There's no evidence so there's no way to seek an arrest warrant. The victim is free to file a criminal complaint, but once you hear out what Mr. Yamaguchi has to say voluntarily, the incident will get sent out to us and that will be the end of it."

The more I thought about it, the stranger it all seemed to me. Was the prosecutor consulted beforehand in every case to determine whether or not the victim should file a criminal complaint?

The prosecutor with whom Mr. A. had consulted was not just anyone—this Prosecutor M. was in a position where he oversaw various others. "I made sure to speak with someone who was high ranking, so there'd be no mistake," Mr. A. said assuredly.

And previously, when I had protested Mr. A.'s negative response, he had said to me in a voice filled with bitterness, "I'm between a rock and a hard place here."

Despite all this, I appreciated Mr. A.'s sense that it was worth bringing in Mr. Yamaguchi for voluntary questioning, that doing so might produce some sort of lead. Though even if Mr. Yamaguchi was willing to speak to the police, there was no chance he'd admit to the rape.

I made up my mind that, before filing the criminal complaint, I would try calling Mr. Yamaguchi. I needed to find out about the possibility of being pregnant, and I thought there was a chance that an unexpected phone call might elicit something about his real intention.

This was not an easy decision. At that point in time, even just the sight of someone who resembled Mr. Yamaguchi sent me into a panic. Would I really be able to speak to him, even when the thought of doing so made me nauseous?

But if I didn't do it, I knew I'd regret it for the rest of my life. My friend K. offered to be there with me, so I plucked up my courage and called Mr. Yamaguchi on his cell phone from her house.

There was no answer. I tried calling once more, right after my first attempt, but he didn't pick up that time either.

But an email arrived soon after.

I no longer have that cell phone. Also, since I've left TBS, you won't be able to reach me at either the branch or the main office. If you are still interested in working in Washington, I will let my successor know.

Please reply to this email address. Thank you.

Y. 04-28-2015, 12:52

It was a strange response. Right after calling his cell phone, he had emailed me saying "I no longer have that cell phone"— what could that mean? These things clearly contradicted each other. And the subject matter was back to business, without answering my questions from the previous email.

There was, however, an important piece of information in the email. Mr. Yamaguchi had said he had left TBS.

That afternoon, I heard from Mr. A. again.

I told him that Mr. Yamaguchi had said he had quit his job, but Mr. A. only scolded me. "You're not supposed to be in direct contact with Mr. Yamaguchi," he said.

"Taking things into your own hands will only make the investigation more difficult. If you want to negotiate directly with Mr. Yamaguchi, then you don't need the police involved, you should speak with a lawyer."

He was probably right. But I couldn't bring myself to just

place all my trust in the police. I wanted to try to collect as much information as possible on my own.

And more than anything else, I needed to know why Mr. Yamaguchi had said there was no possible way I could be pregnant. I didn't remember anything. And yet, whatever had happened had a direct effect on my body. This had been my last chance to get a straight answer before I filed the criminal complaint.

That same day, I reached out to the Sheraton Miyako Hotel about the video footage. The hotel's security cameras deleted old data as they recorded new video, so the evidence would only be available for a given period. I had been told that the time limit was soon approaching, so I felt an urgency to act quickly.

The person in charge of security to whom I spoke said, as might have been expected, that they would not be able to release the video footage without a court order, so all I could do was request that they preserve the data. I had wanted to ensure that this objectively important evidence would be in my possession, but I would have to put my faith in the hotel keeping their promise that they would keep the data.

Filing a Report and Criminal Complaint

On April 30, I went to the Takanawa Police Department and filed a report and a criminal complaint. This required a police record of my statement, so once more, I described what happened, from the beginning and in detail.

Because of my memory loss, I had asked Mr. A. numerous times to investigate the possibility of date-rape drugs.

Of course, that's not actually what they are called. The drugs used are various sleeping pills and sedatives, which have fallen under the moniker of "date-rape drugs." Such ordinary sleeping pills can be bought at any drugstore for five dollars. With no taste or odor, these can be mixed with alcohol, and the victim is raped once she loses consciousness. Such incidents have occurred with enough regularity in the United States that it has become a social issue.

After consuming these drugs, one temporarily loses consciousness and memory for anywhere from two to eight hours, during which time one might behave normally, or seem high or drunk, or experience nausea. The victim won't have any recollection of this.

I have a very high tolerance for alcohol. I always end up looking after my drunk friends. I have never passed out after drinking that quantity of alcohol. My physical condition at the time of the attack wasn't any different from usual.

I knew Mr. A. would tell me that, at this point in time, there was no evidence, but for my own reasons, I wanted him to understand this fact, so on the day I filed the report, I brought up date-rape drugs once more.

He said the same thing as when I first met him, that too much time had passed and there was no way to test whether date-rape drugs had been used. But this time he also told me, "Unlike with junkies, if you take sleeping pills once, there's almost no trace left in the body or in the hair follicles, so even if you were tested now, it would still be useless."

So that meant there was no way to test conclusively for evidence that date-rape drugs had been used. I thought about this as I signed the report and the criminal complaint.

I had assumed that, if I went to the police, the facts would become clear and they would investigate my claim. But that isn't what happened. No matter how many times I told the same story, the response was always "There's no easy way" or "It's tough." The "facts" had proven to be elusive.

Nevertheless, I knew that I had no choice but to gather these facts, one by one, and assemble them to be presented together.

CHAPTER FOUR
OFFENSE AND DEFENSE

Where Was Mr. Yamaguchi?

TBS had contacted the police, saying that Mr. Yamaguchi had returned to Japan from the US on April 27. Because of his fifteen-day suspension, he wouldn't be at work through May 14; and on May 15, he would be back in Washington for the handover to his successor, and then was scheduled to begin working in the sales department in Tokyo on June 16.

The Japanese police could not conduct their questioning in Washington.

It was impossible to predict what Mr. Yamaguchi's plans were—would he remain with TBS as a salesman? Or would he quit, as he himself had said?

And what would be the best timeframe for the voluntary questioning? In Mr. A.'s opinion, the sooner the better, but here they stood to waste an unnecessary month and a half.

Anyway, Mr. Yamaguchi had told me that he had left TBS, that he couldn't be reached there, and that he no longer had that cell phone, so there was no way of contacting him.

Amid these frustrations, I learned that Mr. Yamaguchi had written on Facebook, "I'm looking at the sea in Izu." It had been included in a post, dated May 1 and titled "The Elements I'm Made Of." There were also posts with photos of Izu on May 3 and 4.

This was the middle of the Golden Week holiday. My friend I. had looked on Mr. Yamaguchi's Facebook page for me. I had been avoiding him myself on social media, so as not to create other problems.

I contacted Mr. A. immediately. If Mr. Yamaguchi were really in Japan, then couldn't he be questioned now? But Mr. A. told me that the police were not able to contact suspects through Facebook or over email. Investigators were prohibited from creating accounts using their own names—it was dangerous for their identities to be revealed—and even when they did create them, a supervisor's approval was required. Also, since this was a holiday week, a quick decision would not be forthcoming.

"Right now we don't know whether Mr. Yamaguchi is really in Japan. Let's not bother with unreliable information," Mr. A. said.

But Mr. A. had said something similar the last time, when news of Mr. Yamaguchi's demotion had appeared in a newspaper's publication. Of course I could understand there might be limitations to the investigation, including capacity issues, but in this digital age, didn't it seem ridiculously analog that the police wouldn't be able to communicate by any means other than the telephone? They couldn't even check this Facebook post from a computer within the police department.

What was more, Mr. A. said, the police would have to inquire with the telephone company about Mr. Yamaguchi's phone number by mail, and their response would take place by mail too. This being Golden Week, there was no way to know how long it would take to hear back. I recognized nothing could be done without an arrest warrant, but I was stunned by how outdated this whole process seemed. Despite the fact that, for victims, there was no time to lose in these matters, just what era were we in if the only way to investigate was by post?

I broached the subject of whether I ought to contact Mr. Yamaguchi directly myself, to find out the best way to reach him.

"That's a difficult issue, as far as the police are concerned—for us to put a victim in direct dialogue with the suspect. It's also likely to influence the investigation." Mr. A. seemed reluctant, but if this were to go on, and if Mr. Yamaguchi were in fact in Japan now, he would most likely soon return to the United States. "But it's probably the only way," Mr. A. conceded.

In the end, Mr. A. authorized me to contact Mr. Yamaguchi, promising that if there were ever any problems with the fact that I had done so, he would testify that it was at the request of the police.

From Mr. A.'s point of view, it must have been a disgrace that the police had to ask a victim to do such things. But if they were required to obtain a final decision from above for every single step in their investigation, especially during the break over Golden Week, then there was simply no way for any swift change of course. I was very grateful that

Mr. A. had accepted my suggestion and agreed to let me go forward.

A Voice I Didn't Want to Hear

After that, I sent the following email to Mr. Yamaguchi, from the lawyer's office and with the lawyer present. I was resistant to including anything about work, but up until this point, the only times Mr. Yamaguchi had responded willingly were to business matters. The lawyer advised me to choose words that make it easy for him to respond.

> *I need to speak with you as soon as possible about pregnancy and work. Please let me know how to reach you.*
> S. 05-04-2015, 11:45

My phone rang right away. The call came from an anonymous number—because Mr. Yamaguchi didn't have a cell phone, he was calling from a public phone, he said.

"You're in Izu, aren't you?" I asked. "I'd like to see you while you're in Japan."

"I return to America tomorrow so there's no way," he said.

"What time is your flight?" I asked.

He paused a moment, then hedged, "I'm on a morning flight." He told me he would call again and hung up.

I was so exhausted from that brief call I felt on the verge of collapse. Ever since that day, I had only emailed with him, and now, being in closer proximity, I went pale and was overcome with nausea. This time, hearing his voice required me to acknowledge his existence more acutely. Our conversation had lasted less than a minute, yet I had the sensation of all my strength leaving my body. I never wanted to hear his voice again.

Nevertheless, it occurred to me that I could go to the Takanawa Police Department and try to speak to him on the phone again, this time in the presence of Mr. A. When Mr. Yamaguchi called back, I could simply hand the phone to Mr. A., who would speak with him about the questioning. It seemed like the fastest way.

I contacted Mr. A. He responded that there was an emergency, someone had fallen into a river, the police had been called, he was unavailable.

What timing, I thought. And was there no one else who could take his place? I finally had confirmation from Mr. Yamaguchi himself that he was in Japan, and this was our chance to take the next step.

But there probably wasn't another investigator who would go about my investigation in the same way.

I sent Mr. Yamaguchi an email anyway.

The hospitals are closed today for the holiday. I might be pregnant, so would you consider extending your stay?
S. 05-04-2015, 14:36

I left the lawyer's office and got on the train, and just as I came out of the station at Yoyogi-Uehara, my phone rang again, from another anonymous number. Since the police weren't available, there was no need for me to speak to him directly, so I didn't answer. A little while later, he replied to my email.

I telephoned you, but since you didn't pick up, I will ring you again soon.
  There's no way I can change my plans tomorrow, but a week from now I will be back in Japan for about two weeks. Nevertheless, I'll do whatever I can, no matter where I am, so please don't hesitate to ask.

Y. 05-04-2015, 15:08

At the time, I was physically and emotionally exhausted from calling Mr. Yamaguchi, and I knew the police wouldn't be taking action that day. On my way to a picnic in the park that my friend K. was taking me to, I sent him an email.

I'm with my family now, so I can't answer the phone.
  I'd like to speak to you in person, so please email me once you know the date you will return to Japan.

S. 05-04-2015, 18:08

For two days, there was no reply.
  It wouldn't be long before Mr. Yamaguchi heard that there was a police investigation. This was my last chance. I would take things a step further. I consulted with my friend and sent the following email.

Dear Mr. Yamaguchi,
Up to now I have tried my best to manage the memories I have and to contain my emotions. Because I think I would

break down if I had to face you. But it has simply become too difficult to contain myself.

That night, I suffered physical and emotional damage as a result of coercive sexual intercourse while I was unconscious.

For several days afterward my vagina was sore, and my nipples were so tender that I couldn't stand under the shower. My knee was dislocated—even today, I am still wearing a knee brace. That you would do something like that to me, after I put my trust in you, was such a shock that I can't sleep at night, and I can no longer go to work. Thinking of my future, I have tried desperately to put a lid on this and move on. But currently, my period is considerably late, and it seems more and more likely that I am pregnant. I must now take swift and practical measures, and if I do not imminently receive from you a wholehearted apology and an explanation of how you will address my work situation and the pregnancy, it will push me to my mental limits and I will have no choice but to seek assistance from those around me. Under normal circumstances, this ought to have already been dealt with—I should have gone to the hospital right away and done what was necessary—but you said that you would return to Japan in a week or two. You need to come back here now. And when you do, please get a cell phone. It is unacceptable not to be able to contact you directly.

I request that you to respond to everything included here. These previous emails where you have ignored or denied parts of what I have said can't go on any longer.

S. 05-06-2015, 22:28

A reply arrived within an hour.

I'm very concerned about the mental and physical exhaustion you describe. And I'm sorry to hear that you don't have anyone close to you in whom you can confide. I am not running away or hiding from you—I will do whatever I can to help, so please relax.

I highly regard your abilities, and I want to do everything I can to support you finding a suitable job in the US. In fact, several concrete offers have come in. In order to move forward to that stage, you must first relax—don't you think you ought to take a more positive outlook?

As for acknowledging the facts, you must calm down. I mean, is it my fault that your knee hurts? You fell asleep while locked in the bathroom at the sushi restaurant. Don't you remember that someone who worked there had to unlock the door from the outside to get you out? According to them, you had collapsed on the toilet, slumped over in an awkward position, so isn't it likely that you injured your knee then? If you're going to insist that I am the one who injured your knee, then will you please explain the situation in which that occurred? And for a number of reasons, I need for you to first calm down.

I'll say it again, I have the best intentions, and I am prepared to do whatever I can to make you feel better, both physically and mentally. We can work together to find a solution to these problems, but first I need you to relax.

And then, please tell me what it is you want from me. What are all of these things that you say I must respond to? I really don't know what you're talking about in your email. I never had any intention of deceiving you or running away. You need to stop being so combative, and tell me clearly and constructively how to sort this out.

Y. 05-06-2015, 23:12

The following morning, another message arrived.

> *In response to the questions in your email, first I am contact-*
> *ing you about how to contact me.*
>
> *At the moment, I am temporarily without an address in*
> *either Japan or the US, so I'm not able to sign a cell phone*
> *contract. If by some means I manage to get a cell phone, I*
> *will let you know as soon as possible. In the meantime, if*
> *you email me, I will respond right away.*
>
> *Up to now, whenever you have emailed me, I have*
> *quickly responded, then found a pay phone and called you.*
> *The day before yesterday, I was driving on the highway when*
> *your email came in, so I immediately got off the highway*
> *and called you from a pay phone. But you didn't answer. I'm*
> *not running away or deceiving you—please be assured that*
> *you can always reach me.*
>
> Y. 05-07-2015, 09:33

Later that afternoon, I responded.

> *Please inform me of the date when you will return to Japan,*
> *the contact information for where you will be staying, as well*
> *as for where you are staying now. This is in order to let you*
> *know as soon as I've seen a doctor. I can't go to the hospital*
> *until you have confirmed this information.*
>
> *You say that you are not running away or hiding—if so,*
> *please disclose these details and promptly return to Japan. I*
> *am being calm. How dare you say that to a woman who has*
> *been raped and might now be pregnant?*
>
> S. 05-07-2015, 15:38

His reply came an hour later.

What do you mean, rape?
I absolutely won't accept that.
If you want to fight this legally, go ahead.
I have absolutely no problem with that.
The next time we meet, I'll bring my lawyer.
Even if you claim it was quasi-rape, there's no way you'll win.
I have plenty of witnesses.
But if you want to fight this, I'll be prepared.
If you're willing to talk this over properly and constructively, perhaps you should adopt a more open-minded attitude. I leave it all up to you.

Y. 05-07-2015, 16:37

This was the first time I had used the word "rape." It was only a matter of time before he realized that I had been to the police, so I had decided to fling it directly at him. But before I could respond, another email arrived, about twenty minutes later.

I have no intention of attacking you or causing you pain. I will spare no effort in doing whatever I can in order for us to move beyond this matter as quickly as possible.

But, if you persist in treating me with such hostility, I will no longer have any option but to respond accordingly. I will stand trial in court for as many months as it takes to clear these baseless charges. It will be your choice whether to do something that will consume and do harm to both of us.

Are you willing to discuss this calmly and constructively?
If so, I will make an early return to Japan.

Y. 05-07-2015, 17:00

During this time, I had been consulting with the lawyer. He remarked upon the point that Mr. Yamaguchi had used the legal term "quasi-rape"—even though I had said nothing about it myself. As previously mentioned, this is the crime that applies in cases when the victim is unconscious due to any kind of drugs or alcohol.

It's not a word that everyone knows or that is common knowledge, but it was worth noting the fact that, as a journalist, Mr. Yamaguchi acknowledged it fit this situation.

The timing of his email replies was also significant. At that time of year, the US was thirteen hours behind Japan—a day-night reversal, plus one hour. Two o'clock in the afternoon in Japan was one o'clock in the morning on the east coast of the US. But even when I sent emails in the middle of the day in my time zone, generally I got a reply within an hour or so.

Could this mean that he really was in Japan?

I called Mr. A. the following day to report this to him. In response to when I told him that I had been consulting with a lawyer about the wording of the emails, Mr. A. said, "If you're talking to a lawyer, are you in talks to pursue a settlement? If so, you may as well stop working with the police."

Mr. A. said he would confer with the public prosecutor, but he knew there were limits to the criminal case and the prosecutor had told him from the start it would be difficult.

"You can tell the lawyer that the police said this," he even suggested.

And then he reiterated, "The emails are of no use."

But it was clear we had made progress with the emails. I had wanted to consult with Mr. A. about the fact that Mr. Yamaguchi had said that he would arrange time to meet with me. Naturally, I thought that would be the perfect chance for the police to conduct their questioning. My intention was to cooperate with the investigation as best I could. That being the case, shouldn't the police have figured out the quickest way to contact Mr. Yamaguchi and done so themselves? I was utterly stunned by their passivity and negative attitude to any kind of progress.

That day, I was supposed to bring the receipts for my medical expenses to the police. "While you're at it, please bring copies of your emails too," Mr. A. said, but I was feeling less inclined about going to see the police.

Why was it that, every time there was a new advance in the case, the investigation seemed to retreat? As I was talking with Mr. A., I finally broke down in tears.

The lawyer had urged me that, if I didn't reply to Mr. Yamaguchi, he would sense that something was underway. Mr. A. suggested that it would be fine to respond briefly that I was taking things into consideration.

I ended the conversation with Mr. A. and then sent an email to Mr. Yamaguchi.

As I've said many times already, right now my health is of utmost concern, so please let me think about it.

S. 05-08-2015, 13:24

It was the middle of the night in the United States, but there was an immediate reply.

I understand. I will adhere to your schedule as best I can. Please contact me at your convenience.

Y. 05-08-2015, 13:53

The Police Aren't Investigating Whether He's Left the Country?

The fact of the matter was, I had no choice but to contact Mr. Yamaguchi directly myself, no matter how agonizing it was for me. I had pushed through the pain for the purpose of obtaining Mr. Yamaguchi's contact information, without which the investigation could not proceed, so that the police would be able to ask him to fill in the gaps in my memory when I had been unconscious. And I had made progress.

Which is why I was so shocked when Mr. A. then asked me about accepting an out-of-court settlement. It made me wonder whether, going forward, I could really place my trust in the police.

Later, Mr. A. contacted me again. "As a police officer, we inform everyone that they might consider an out-of-court settlement. My own stance hasn't changed since the beginning—once you have filed a criminal complaint, the police will do what is necessary, no matter the obstacles. Regardless, we will proceed according to plan."

I had no reason to think that Mr. A. was lying, but if that was the case, then why had the public prosecutor said early on that it would be impossible to seek an arrest warrant? Thinking about the institution of the police, my doubts only seemed to grow.

I had an uncle who was a former public prosecutor. I decided I would speak to him about the questions I had about the prosecutor's and the police's actions.

The first thing my uncle told me was that if the security video clearly showed the unusual circumstances of me being dragged into the hotel, the typical protocol would be to question the other party about what happened. Whether it merited that an investigation be opened would depend upon those facts, he said. He also said that, as the victim in the case, I could ask to see the results of the police's inquiries at the restaurant where we had eaten.

When I talked about how Mr. Yamaguchi said he was abroad but that he was likely in Japan, my uncle said that airline travel and passport information could be verified with the Ministry of Foreign Affairs, that it was possible to find out the next day whether or not he had gone abroad. And even if it took longer, determining whether or not he had been in a foreign country as of today was relatively straightforward. "The police aren't investigating whether he's left the country?" he asked.

As an alum of the prosecutor's office, my uncle declared that it was impossible for them to have concluded from the start that they couldn't arrest him, or that even with a voluntary interrogation the case was certain to be dropped. Even if they couldn't arrest him with the evidence they had at the time, it was possible that more would be discovered in the course of an investigation. Let alone the fact that, if he was arrested, there would likely be major breakthroughs in the investigation, so there was no reason to decide from the start that it would be dismissed. "Have more faith in the police and the prosecutor," my uncle said. He also encouraged me to continue to consult with the lawyer.

To be sure, even if they built a criminal case and brought charges against Mr. Yamaguchi, the crime had taken place behind closed doors, and the trial would predictably be intense. But that all depended upon the investigation, and it seemed inconceivable that any case would be deemed nonprosecutable from the start.

And yet, this begged the question: Why were the police so unmotivated to pursue the investigation?

Regardless, I had no choice but to rely on them. I pulled myself back together again, knowing I had to prepare for the questioning. I also sent another message to Mr. Yamaguchi, asking him about the thing I was most desperate to know. Seeing that I couldn't place full confidence in what the police would do, I felt I had to try to get a straight answer from Mr. Yamaguchi before they intervened.

When I think about what transpired next, I know that this was the right decision.

"I Have This Ailment, You See."

In your messages, you keep saying that you are not running away or hiding, and yet for many days now, you have not responded to the issue that is most critical to me. This does nothing to assuage my fears and I can't help but feel that you are only protecting yourself.

You stated that it was not possible I could be pregnant— what did you mean by this?

You have said repeatedly that you will do whatever you can, but just what is the exact meaning of this "whatever you can"?

S. 05-08-2015, 19:06

I received a reply about two hours later.

If there is a critical answer that you have not received, please inform me what that is. I will respond right away.

Y. 05-08-2015, 21:37

You stated that it was not possible I could be pregnant— why not?

S. 05-08-2015, 22:57

The answer arrived a few minutes later.

I have this ailment, you see.

Y. 05-08-2015, 23:05

What ailment? Please be more specific, since this affects my own health.

S. 05-08-2015, 23:09

The ailment I speak of is low sperm motility.

Y. 05-08-2015, 23:12

In these two emails, as well as in the responses I'd previously received, Mr. Yamaguchi had acknowledged that he had had sexual intercourse with me. But I was confused by the excuse he gave—I knew that he had a son, so it still seemed possible that I could be pregnant.

The messages exchanged thereafter are as follows:

If there are medical measures that require urgent attention, I will cover these—whatever the cost—please provide the details. And then, if you would like to meet to discuss matters, I had suggested returning to Japan temporarily in order to do so, but you never responded clearly to this. You accuse me, without making any concrete demands, so I am at a loss.

I'm very sorry to hear that you are so exhausted, both mentally and physically, and I will do whatever I can to help remedy your condition—please make concrete suggestions as to what should be done.

As for why I have not apologized, this has to do with a fundamentally different understanding of the facts. Even what's written here in these emails deviates considerably from reality. But disputing what you insist is your version of events would only exacerbate your fragile emotional condition, so I don't dare.

That's not to say that I have no interest in apologizing to you. Just that, in circumstances where there is such a fundamental disagreement about the facts, I think it might lead to further misunderstanding and various complications.

I'll say it again, it pains me deeply to hear that you are suffering, with no one to offer you guidance. Please do let me know what it is specifically that I can do for you now.

Y. 05-10-2015, 12:38

99

First and foremost, I want to hear you apologize and express remorse. Just what do you mean by "deviates from reality"? Without an answer to this, I feel that it would be pointless for us to continue having a conversation. Isn't it our job to report the facts? There's nothing I hate more than those who distort the facts.

S. 05-11-2015, 13:40

Regarding my apology and assistance, please go back and reread my email from May 10. Again, I do not wish to discuss with you over email our versions of the facts. I have no intention of responding to your demand that I apologize first. In these circumstances, I think anyone else would react exactly the same way.

This does not mean that I refuse to offer the assistance that you require. Even now, I am prepared to support you with the best intentions. I'll do whatever I can, as long as you tell me what it is you need.

However, if you insist on maintaining this combative and hostile attitude, it will be futile for us to repeat this same direct exchange over and over, and I will request the intervention of a third party in any ongoing contact.

Y. 05-12-2015, 12:45

I wouldn't be able to get him to say anything more. And I had nothing left to offer in response. And then, the following morning, two more emails arrived.

Someone in the Washington-based Japanese media to whom I reached out on behalf of your job search contacted me to say that they would like to interview you.

Regardless of the poor state of communication between us at the moment, if you are interested in working in the US, please do not hesitate to convey your wishes to me.

Y. 05-13-2015, 00:07

You probably don't take me at my word, but I really am concerned about you. I offer you whatever support I can—I still hope that you will tell me exactly what it is you need from me.

Y. 05-13-2015, 10:37

This constitutes the entirety of our email correspondence.

Baffling Testimony from the Sushi Restaurant

The investigation seemed to be progressing. I asked Mr. A. about the interviews he had conducted of the staff at the sushi restaurant, and here is what he said:

"I think you'll be surprised. They say that, between the two of you, you drank almost a whole 1.8-liter magnum and that you didn't order any food besides simple small plates and futomaki rolls. You mostly just drank saké. That being the case, anyone would have been drunk, no matter how high their tolerance."

I was stunned. Had I really had that much to drink? I had no memory beyond a certain point in the night so I couldn't know for sure, but I found it highly improbable.

When I pressed him further, although the staff had said we drank "almost a whole 1.8-liter magnum"—which was equivalent to ordering ten bottles of saké at the sushi restaurant, since saké is traditional served to customers in ceramic vessels of about six ounces each—he said there was no record of an itemized receipt. Even if we had three or four bottles each, that was still a far cry from one 1.8-liter magnum.

When I asked Mr. A. what the staff said about my condition when leaving the restaurant, he told me:

"Do you remember sitting down in another customer's chair? Apparently, you also started up a conversation with a different guest. They said you were walking around the restaurant without your shoes on. Mr. Yamaguchi had to get you to leave. That's how drunk they say you were. One of the staff says he remembers pouring the saké in front of both of you."

I had absolutely no recollection of any of this. Beyond not having any memory of it, I just couldn't believe it. There would be a credit card record of Mr. Yamaguchi having paid the full amount, but then why was there no receipt? Had the restaurant already thrown away the receipts from less than a month and a half ago?

Even if there were no drugs involved, Mr. A. said, the restaurant staff's statement about how much I had drunk met the requirements for quasi-rape. But I refused to accept this. Had it really been only alcohol that I had drunk? If so, then why was there such an abrupt break in my memory after ordering the third bottle of saké?

There was something else that bothered me too.

In one of his emails, Mr. Yamaguchi had written, *You fell asleep while locked in the bathroom at the sushi restaurant. Don't you remember that someone who worked there had to unlock the door from the outside to get you out? According to them, you had collapsed on the toilet, slumped over in an awkward position.*

If I had been drunk and passed out, then how is it possible that I could have sat down and had a conversation with other customers, according to the staff's statement? Can a person who is in that much of a drunken stupor and who has already collapsed get back up again and behave in that manner?

Mr. A. urged me to take a pregnancy test. Despite the fact that I had gotten a prescription for the morning-after pill, there was still no sign of my period and it was long past the time when I expected it. I kept telling myself that it was due to stress or from taking the prescription, but the fact was that it was more than a month late. There had also been abnormal vaginal bleeding.

What if I were pregnant? What would I do? I knew that I ought to be tested, but I was frightened. I couldn't wait too long though. I didn't have the courage to go to a hospital or clinic on my own, so I asked my friend S. to accompany me to get a pregnancy test.

Perhaps due to the extraordinary circumstances, I had completely forgotten about these details until recently when I read the statement S. gave for the Committee for the Inquest of the Prosecution. According to S., even going to the hospital was traumatizing for me; although I had hoped to see a female doctor, only male doctors were available, and so she had come with me into the examination room.

S. said that I had been frightened to go into such a small room with the male doctor, and that I had been extremely anxious, squeezing her hand tightly until receiving the results that I was not pregnant.

I doubt I could have done that on my own. I am grateful to have such close friends around me, and I thank them for the support they have given me.

The Taxi Driver's Testimony

Mr. A. pressed ahead with the investigation of my case.

I learned that he had taken a statement from the taxi driver who had taken Mr. Yamaguchi and me from the sushi restaurant to the hotel. The precise date of the driver's statement was May 13.

From his statement, I learned that I had repeatedly said, "Please let me off at a nearby station"; that, inside the taxi, at first there had been discussion related to work, but I had fallen silent in the midst of this, and when he dropped us off, I could not exit the taxi on my own; and that once I was out of the taxi, there was vomit visible on my clothing.

It was very disturbing to hear someone else describe my actions during a period of which I have no memory, but I was relieved to learn that I had asked to be taken to a train station numerous times. It meant that I had in fact been trying to get myself home all along.

I also found out, from the housekeeping records at the Sheraton Miyako Hotel, that there was no mention of any vomit being discovered in the room. Mr. Yamaguchi had explained in his email that I had thrown up in two places in the room as well as in the bathroom, but the cleaning staff had not noted any areas that required special treatment.

At the same time, this wasn't included in the report, but I found out that the housekeeper in charge of that floor made the following statement: "One of the beds had not been used. And on the other bed, there was blood."

Why wouldn't that detail have made it into the final report?

Supposedly, this housekeeper was a foreigner and she didn't speak Japanese fluently, so someone in charge from the hotel had served as an interpreter. The woman had been uncertain about this part of the story, so the language used to interpret her statement had not been definitive about which room she was referring to. Apparently, it was due to her uncertainty, and the fact that there was no record that the room had required special treatment for removing vomit or odor, that these details had not been included in the report.

Much later, in preparation for my petition to the Committee for the Inquest of the Prosecution to reopen the investigation, I contacted several staff members from the Sheraton Miyako Hotel, requesting to speak with them and take statements. I was, however, rebuffed. Without the hotel's cooperation, it was difficult to know who to ask, or to determine which staff member was in charge of the room in question.

As previously mentioned, I had been told that there was no security camera on the second floor monitoring that part of the hallway where Mr. Yamaguchi was staying. I wondered why a major foreign-financed hotel wouldn't have a hallway security camera. And why wouldn't there be one near the elevators on the same floor?

I also wished that, seeing a person who was unable to walk on her own and who wasn't a hotel guest cross the lobby, someone might have called out, "Is everything all right?" With those few words, what happened that night might have been prevented.

As Mr. A. had pointed out, my limp body was enough of a spectacle to make passersby take notice. When K. and I watched the video, we had both shuddered with nausea. And later the taxi driver said in his statement, "The hotel bellman had looked concerned."

If, as Mr. Yamaguchi said, I was vomiting and unconscious, he ought to have taken me to a hospital or called an ambulance.

Whether due to drugs or alcohol, there are many cases where people die from choking on their vomit when they are unconscious. In fact, a relative of mine lost their life this way.

The Humiliation of the "Reenactment"

In tandem with this progress in the investigation, I was told that the police needed to confirm certain details about the incident. This process of "reenactment," as it is called, often takes place at the scene of the crime. They literally recreate the circumstances of what happened for the purpose of taking photographs.

In my case, it was not possible to do this at the hotel, so

I went to the top floor of the Takanawa Police Department, where there is a judo hall.

There was a blue mat spread out on the floor, and judo uniforms hung along the wall. Many police officers must have trained here—the room smelled of sweat.

Using a life-size doll, in a judo hall filled with only male investigators, I was forced to reenact the circumstances of my rape.

"Lie down there, please," I was told, as I lay face up on the blue mat, surrounded by men. One of the investigators placed a large doll on top of me.

"Like this?" "Or was it more like this?" they asked as they rearranged the doll.

As the camera flashed and I heard the shutter clicking, my mind tensed up and then completely shut down.

Had the same thing happened that night?

"Were you a virgin?" an investigator asked. "It may be difficult for you to answer." Various other police officers had asked me this repeatedly before, and in response to this frequent and ridiculous question, I always replied, "How does that have anything to do with what happened?" All they ever said was, "We have to ask."

Every single investigator I spoke to asked me this same question. But this time, when they asked me, I was unable to offer my standard retort. I was just trying my best to answer their questions.

The fact that victims of sexual assault are forced to endure such humiliation shines a light on the flaws in the investigative system, and the flaws in how investigators are trained as well.

Later, when I told a colleague at Reuters about this, she said, "That was a second rape," and she immediately began reporting on it. This was the single most difficult experience I had with the police, and for some reason, they absolutely refused to allow my friend K. to accompany me. Instead, she had to wait in the reception area on the first floor. The ordeal might have been slightly easier, had she been there with me.

In addition—although this happened later when my case was transferred from the Takanawa Police Department to the Tokyo Metropolitan Police Department's First Investigation Division—two of my friends were asked to give statements about the incident.

K. and S. had known me for a long time, and they were the friends in whom I had confided immediately after the attack. The investigators had asked them about my "type" of man and about my past romantic relationships.

Just how did my past sexual experience or my preference in men have anything to do with the attack, and what connection did it have with the investigation?

Arrest at Narita Airport

Had Mr. A. really done everything he could? It was around mid-May when this thought occurred to me. Mr. Yamaguchi had been in the United States, so there didn't appear to be any further developments.

When I thought about it, there had been so many hoops to jump through even just to file the complaint. I had spent those days doing everything I could possibly think of to get the police to continue the investigation.

During this time, having managed to gradually resume working, I received a job opportunity in Germany. I was still suffering from panic attacks whenever I saw someone who resembled Mr. Yamaguchi, so it was somewhat of a relief to be in Berlin, where there were comparatively fewer Japanese people. I was finally able to return to my own work and a normal lifestyle.

While I was in Germany, I received a call on June 4 saying that Mr. Yamaguchi was going to be arrested at Narita Airport, upon his return to Japan. Hearing the word "arrested" over the phone, I felt as though I were having a strange dream—I couldn't quite grasp that it might be a realistic possibility.

"He's returning from the US on Monday the eighth. The arrest will take place at the airport, once he passes through immigration."

Mr. A. maintained his composure, but there was a trace of excitement in his voice. The purpose of his call was in preparation for the interrogation that would follow the arrest, to request that I return to Japan as well, as soon as possible.

I should have been glad to receive this news.

And yet, I couldn't summon the least bit of happiness. The moment the call ended, it felt as though I lost all sensation in my body. What lay in store for me now? I felt a wave of exhaustion, imagining the offensive backlash I could expect from Mr. Yamaguchi and those in his circle.

Just when I had managed to resume my own life, this attack and its aftermath was about to drag me back down.

But I had to pull myself together. The time had come for the truth to come to light. I made the necessary arrangements to cover my work, and I started looking for a return ticket to Japan.

Up until now, Mr. A. had repeatedly referred to the "benefit of the doubt"—the principle of "innocent until proven guilty." He had told me that a person can't be charged with a crime based on suspicion alone, without evidence. The most heartening fact here was that the police must have gathered enough evidence and testimony for the court to authorize a request for the arrest warrant.

A Shocking Phone Call

Four days later—on the day the arrest was scheduled to take place—I received another call from Mr. A. Of course, I expected to hear that Mr. Yamaguchi had been arrested, but when I answered the phone, Mr. A.'s voice was bleak as he said my name.

"Ms. Ito, we were not, in fact, able to arrest him. We were prepared to do so. I was ready to go, but at the last minute we were ordered to stop. I am truly sorry for my own inadequacy. I'm being taken off the case; I will no longer be in charge. Until they assign my successor, please be in contact with my supervisor."

I was surprised and disappointed, yet a part of me had expected this all along. Questions surged up, one after another.

Why did this happen now? Something wasn't right.

"The prosecution granted the request for the arrest warrant, the court authorized it, didn't they? How can something that's been decided be overturned so easily?" I asked.

The answer was astonishing. "The stop order came from MPD, from the top." He was referring to the Tokyo Metropolitan Police Department.

It was impossible. How could the police put a halt to the activities of the prosecution that was controlling the investigation of the case?

"Does this kind of thing happen often? I mean, the police stepping in?" I asked.

"In rare exceptions. Hardly any cases."

I kept repeating the same questions, and Mr. A. said, "The new person in charge of handling the case will explain this to you. And it's likely my phone number will change after this, but when you're back in Japan, I'd like to meet with you to talk things over."

His cell phone number would change? What was going to happen to Mr. A.?

"Will you be okay, Mr. A.?"

"I haven't committed a fireable offense, so I should be fine."

He apologized profusely and, no matter what question I asked, the only reply he gave was, "I hope you can pardon my failure."

"I just can't understand."

Before now, Mr. A. had told me many times, "If you're going to involve yourself in the investigation like this, why not do it yourself? You don't need the police, do you?" But I had relied on them; I had placed absolute trust in the police and cooperated fully. Had I not done so, I would have lost my nerve, and now I had learned the hard way that I wasn't being taken seriously anyway.

But having come this far, those things no longer mattered.

"I just don't get it," I repeated.

Mr. A. said, "Neither do I."

Mr. A. had been the one who would have confirmed Mr. Yamaguchi's identity, and he must have seen him pass right before his eyes.

My sense of powerlessness—that it didn't matter what we did—merged with my fear and loneliness that there was no one left to trust within the police force. I felt frustrated by my own insignificance. All of these thoughts and all of my exhaustion erupted within me, and the sobs welled up in waves.

I kept questioning him further, but Mr. A. would not tell me anything about why the arrest had been stopped. Would the new person who took over after him be any different? "Probably not" was his reply.

For the past two months, Mr. A. had devoted a tremendous amount of time to the investigation of this case and had persevered, even while being caught between my insistence and the pressure from his superiors. Who would take his place now? Would I be back at square one, forced to tell the same story over and over again to a new investigator?

Mr. A. and I may have argued with each other, but he had diligently kept up the investigation. The fact that he had been taken off the case was a huge shock to me, more than the arrest being called off.

The last thing he said over the phone was to repeat, "I'm sorry for my inadequacy."

All I could manage to stammer was "Thank you very much. You worked very hard. Take care of yourself." Before hanging up, I added that I was sorry this incident had had a negative effect on his career as well. Although up until that point we had been in opposition as victim and investigator, I felt saddened, as if I were bidding a sudden farewell to a comrade in arms.

My tears spilled over with all of these inexpressible emotions. I felt weak, at a loss, completely alone on a residential street in Berlin. Every path forward seemed to have been blocked. Here I was, just one small person, up against this unseen force that I couldn't even properly confront.

A decision from the top of Tokyo's MPD. From just that, I already knew that one single investigator and one victim would never learn the truth.

There had to be some other way to go about it.

Who should I ask? This question kept running through my mind.

I returned immediately to my friend's place where I was staying in Germany, and I made a phone call from the kitchen. I wanted to try to reach Prosecutor M., who had been in charge of the case.

The person who answered told me that Prosecutor M. had been taken off the case. Him too. On the day when the stop order for the arrest had been issued, both the investigator and the prosecutor in charge were removed—everyone was gone.

The kitchen was drenched in afternoon light, and as I stared at a basket filled with fruit and vegetables, I realized that I needed to get back to Tokyo where I could seek out the truth as soon as I could, but a part of me was still glad not to be in Japan.

It was a clear and crisp day. Not the usual overcast Berlin sky—the weather was quite fine. It was the one thing that saved me, at least, on that day when I got the call.

Mr. Yamaguchi hadn't been arrested, and he would still be working at TBS's main office. If I went back to work at Reuters in Japan, my office would be in the building directly across from where he was. I couldn't bear the idea of going back there.

CHAPTER FIVE
CASE DISMISSED

I immediately canceled my plans to return to Japan from Germany and decided instead to leave for Israel to visit a friend and former roommate. At the very least I could exercise under the hot sun and dedicate myself to taking photographs. As I was walking through the Old City in Jerusalem, I received a call from Mr. A.'s supervisor in the Takanawa Police Department.

He informed me that MPD's First Investigation Division would be taking over the case. First Investigation also wanted to speak with me directly but had been unable to do so as of yet because of the time difference.

Did that mean they still intended to investigate the case? But, how?

After all, there was no chance of arresting Mr. Yamaguchi, was there?

When I finally spoke with the investigator at MPD in charge of the case, I didn't get a proper explanation to any of my questions.

For example, why hadn't the arrest been carried out?

The only response I received was "In order to conduct

further investigation." But for two months the investigation had exhausted every conceivable possibility. The police's last resort had been to arrest Mr. Yamaguchi in order to forcibly search his laptop for files that might have been recorded there, or any other evidence, before it could be destroyed.

I contacted my uncle, the former prosecutor. He was well versed in the ways that an arrest warrant was handled, and his explanation would prove to be very useful. My uncle told me that once a court had authorized an arrest warrant, it was no simple matter not to carry it out. He advised me to go to MPD with a lawyer present and to inquire about the current status of the arrest warrant.

First Investigation's Nonsensical Explanation

As soon as I was back in Japan, I was summoned by MPD. I was introduced to the new members of the unit in charge of my case. That day the main people I met with was a female detective from First Investigation and her male supervisor. They said that a team of about four or five people would be investigating my case.

This was an entirely different staff lineup from the officers at the Takanawa Police Department, who had already conducted an investigation of everything that could be done voluntarily. And the explanation these two offered me during our meeting was nonsensical.

Since no weapon had been used, they weren't concerned that Mr. Yamaguchi would destroy evidence. Once arrested, he could only be held in custody for twenty days, and since the scope of evidence that was known at the time wasn't enough for a conviction, even if they went to the trouble of arresting Mr. Yamaguchi, the case would end up being dismissed. For these reasons, they explained, the investigation would have to continue a bit further on a voluntary basis.

But then why had they requested the arrest warrant? And why had the court granted it? Their explanation made no sense.

When I asked them specifically how the scope of the investigation would be expanded, their response was "We will discuss the testimonies we have more thoroughly along with other items." They didn't offer anything conclusive at all.

In particular, with regard to the arrest warrant, they had no convincing answers despite my repeated questions about it. Here is what the male investigator had to say:

"Arrest warrants are easy to come by. All it takes is for there to be a victim, then the victim says, 'That person is the perpetrator.' We investigate to a certain extent and say, 'Hmm, could be'—and there you have it. In this instance, especially, you were acquainted with Mr. Yamaguchi, so there was a zero percent chance that you were mistaking him for someone else. It may sound horrible, but most of the time, that's enough to issue an arrest warrant.

"Before an arrest warrant is carried out, the investigator must determine whether or not the necessary conditions to make the arrest have been met, whether enforcing it will be fair—this must be considered once again.

"What often happens is that the suspect is out of the country, or his whereabouts are unknown—cases where he may not be on the run but we don't know where he is—so the officer obtains an arrest warrant to have on hand. Just because we have it doesn't mean that we're obliged to carry it out. It means that when it reaches the stage of carrying it out, the officer must again decide what's best.

"Even in your case, I believe that it was right to have obtained the warrant, because Mr. Yamaguchi was in the United States, but once he returned, there was no fear of not knowing his whereabouts or that he would flee. In particular, since there was no concern that he would destroy evidence, the question became: Is it reasonable to arrest him?

"And another thing to consider is, how does a person's social status relate to the investigation? That is to say, frankly, it does relate. Someone with a certain social standing, you always know where to find them, they have a family and a network of people surrounding them—there's no risk of flight. For that reason, it's not necessary to arrest them.

"The Takanawa Police Department may have made the decision to obtain an arrest warrant, but we are their supervising division, and when the report came in, I believe that the response that was issued was, 'This does not currently meet the necessary conditions for arrest, so stand down.'"

His response raised numerous doubts.

First, even if it were plausible to obtain an arrest warrant to keep on hand, in this case, nothing about doing so had been simple. Mr. A. had said early on that the public prosecutor had told him it would be impossible to get an arrest warrant. But after evidence such as eyewitness testimony and security camera footage steadily accumulated, that assessment was overturned.

Second, on what grounds could they maintain there was no concern that Mr. Yamaguchi would destroy evidence? What about the video that had potentially been recorded on his laptop?

And anyway, the officer's argument made it seem as if a person with social status didn't do things like destroy evidence or flee. Was that to imply, then, that someone with no social standing might destroy evidence or attempt to run away? Did that mean it was easy to arrest someone with little or no social status?

Wouldn't that indicate that people with high social standing received preferential treatment?

But no matter how highly respected someone was, they were still human. They still made mistakes.

And over email Mr. Yamaguchi had claimed that he didn't have an address in the US or in Japan, and that he no longer worked for TBS. Even if that were a lie, he was the one who volunteered that he was currently homeless and unemployed. Just whose standards were being used here? If MPD investigators were making decisions and statements such as this, could it still be said that Japan was governed by the rule of law?

Third, MPD was the supervising division, so why had their decision that "there was no fear of flight so it wasn't necessary to arrest him" been made on the same day he was to be arrested, after officers had already been deployed to the scene?

Had MPD not been receiving any reports from the Takanawa Police prior to that day?

Advised by the Police to
Seek a Lawyer for a Settlement

The officer had more to say.

"Mr. Yamaguchi's lawyer paid me a visit today. He had something he wanted me to relay to you—is it all right if I tell you now?

"He had only one thing to say, that he would like to negotiate for an out-of-court settlement, and asked if he might contact your lawyer. This is merely my advice, but you should not negotiate with him directly—it's better to do everything through a lawyer.

"In a situation such as this, it's only ever about money.

"Rape and quasi-rape are crimes that require a formal complaint, so it cannot be prosecuted unless the victim presses charges, even if we know who the perpetrator is. In such cases, if the victim were looking for an out-of-court settlement, the other party would probably insist that the charges be withdrawn. From the accused's point of view, once a case has been dismissed, there's not much need for an out-of-court settlement. For their part, they would want to make an arrangement before a decision is made about whether or not to indict.

"Of course, a civil case and a criminal case are different things—just because a criminal case is dismissed doesn't mean that the victim can't win a civil case. Although, it would be likely to make the defense feel they were in a stronger position.

"I apologize for putting all this on you at once. Have you spoken with a lawyer? We know one who specializes in representing victims, and if you retain them, their services are essentially free—they're covered by public funds.

"If you're uncomfortable, an investigator can accompany you. It can take time, from when you request a lawyer to when they are appointed, so may I ask for your response today so that we can proceed?"

I hadn't given any thought to an out-of-court settlement. But I had hustled to find a lawyer. A friend had recommended someone who I had been consulting with at the time—he had offered me various advice and had yet to charge me anything. I was extremely grateful for his help, but he had a connection with TBS, so he had told me that if the case went to court, he wouldn't be able to represent me.

Since there was a system for retaining a lawyer free of charge, I consented to meeting with the person the police knew. It seemed odd how keen they were about advising me to seek a settlement, but I needed a lawyer who could help me press MPD for more information about the arrest warrant. At the time, I wasn't thinking much further beyond that.

The investigators reassured me that, on their end, they would be continuing the investigation.

On June 22, the results of the DNA analysis came back, indicating that Mr. Yamaguchi's DNA had been found on my bra. DNA material matching Mr. Yamaguchi's Y chromosomes had been detected on the strap, the interior and exterior of the cup, and on the hooks.

Then they conducted a search of Mr. Yamaguchi's home, during which they seized any computers or tablets.

Mr. Yamaguchi was questioned and he took a polygraph, but nothing unordinary was detected.

When the police analyzed his computer, they said the model had no internal camera and showed no sign of having had an external device installed. Nor were there any files—images or videos—on the computer related to the incident.

I wondered how they could be so sure that there weren't "any images or videos." Would they really have been able to confirm that through an investigation that wasn't compulsory? And how could they be sure that the computer they confiscated was the same one that had been at the scene?

This only increased my doubts.

And now that the case had been taken over by MPD's First Investigation, I had to file a report all over again. Ostensibly this was so that any additional details could be included, but as far as the case was concerned, why couldn't they use the report that had been filed at the Takanawa Police Department? I had lost count of how many times I'd told the story, but I started from the beginning, once again.

Going to the Lawyer's Office in a Police Car

Several days later, I returned to MPD to corroborate the text of the report that had been filed. This process took some time, and in the midst of it, the police and I ended up going to see the lawyer who they had previously mentioned to me. The appointment had already been made. We could continue the corroboration afterward, the investigator told me, or it was fine to finish it another day.

I was driven to the lawyer's office in a police car. I would have expected that I would go to the meeting by myself, but for some reason, several investigators accompanied me in the car.

At the time, my number-one objective in seeking a lawyer was to find out the status of the arrest warrant that Mr. A. had obtained. Since both Mr. Yamaguchi and myself had been abroad, there was reason to believe that the warrant would remain in effect, that it wouldn't have expired. I needed a lawyer who would go with me to the police and question them about the status of the arrest warrant and how long it was valid for. This had been what my uncle, the former prosecutor, had advised me to do.

At the office of the female lawyer to whom I was introduced by the police, I was again questioned about the attack. The investigators were present the whole time as I recounted the full details. Since I couldn't very well ask the lawyer whether she'd be able to help me inquire about the warrant while they were there, I asked them to leave the room.

Apparently this lawyer did indeed specialize in out-of-court settlements. After the investigators left, I tentatively expressed the doubts I was feeling about the police's investigation, but I didn't get much of a response from her.

It dawned on me that it wouldn't be prudent to speak to her any further of my doubts about the police or the warrant. I had been brought in a police car to see a lawyer who had been recommended by the police, and the investigators had stayed very close, listening in as this lawyer had discussed an out-of-court settlement with me, only leaving when I asked them to. I finally realized how odd this was.

Nothing surprised me anymore. But a part of me still

wanted to trust the authorities and the investigators working my case.

The lawyer told me about the various out-of-court settlements that she had handled. According to her, the best outcome was when the other party acknowledged guilt and paid consolation money.

In this instance, the settlement that Mr. Yamaguchi had proposed was likely an inducement to withdraw the report and complaint.

"When an out-of-court settlement is reached, a document is drawn up. You can either demand that the opening statement include an apology, or request no apology and only money. And the amount of the settlement is often in the range of a million yen," she continued to explain.

So there were settlements that didn't include an apology? That was hard to imagine. With the money paid, the facts were sealed and not to be spoken of.

And, I wondered, who had decided upon this amount of a million yen? The tremendous impact that this sexual assault would have on the rest of my life, the amount of time it would consume, the medical expenses—the total cost was incalculable. And above all, time and mental anguish were not things I could put a price on.

And yet, according to the lawyer, many cases were settled for this paltry sum. The reason was that, within Japan's legal system, it was quite difficult for sexual crimes to be brought to justice. And then, the experience of the investigation process and appearing in court also caused significant distress.

During the course of the investigation, I had heard about

"sex crime trial observer mania," which referred to the people who, on days when the court was hearing sexual crimes, lined up early in the morning to get a seat in the gallery.

Going to court myself, having to confront and speak to my assailant whose face I had tried forget, and then the gallery filled with curious onlookers—the mere thought of them all staring at me made the blood drain from my face.

Since a revision to the Criminal Procedure Code in 2000, victims testifying in court are permitted to do so behind a partition, so as not to have to be face-to-face with their assailant—sometimes even testifying from a separate room. But many victims still fear intimidation and retaliation from their assailants.

This was why even the police said it was better to resolve things with money, before things got too ugly. I wondered how many women had, up to this day, been silenced like this? In 35.4 percent of sexual crimes cases in Japan, the victims withdrew their complaints after settlements or negotiations (this figure is from 2010). The fact was that, for various reasons, one third of victims agreed to out-of-court settlements. And among them were cases where the assailant had video evidence of the assault and promised to destroy it once the complaint was withdrawn.

"It seems likely that you will ask me to negotiate a settlement for you," the lawyer concluded.

But I hadn't said a single word about wanting to settle. Was a settlement the only option for a victim within this system, if they retained a lawyer whose fees were covered by public funds?

At MPD, the police had told me how they refer people to

lawyers who specialized in representing victims. The male investigator on my case had said this:

"There are lawyers who only represent victims, who do not practice criminal law. If you retain one of them, it's essentially free—their services are covered by public funds. This is part of a new system. We have had many victims take advantage of these services—on the whole, they are trustworthy people."

What he meant was that lawyers who practice criminal law represent the accused. But the woman sitting before me now had told me about a case in which she represented the suspect in a settlement—despite the fact that she supposedly specialized in only representing victims.

What did all of this mean? Why were the police going to such lengths to have me settle out of court?

In the three months since the attack, I had been unable to carry on with my work normally. Due to the injury to my right knee, which seemed to have been sustained during the struggle the night of the incident, it was impossible for me to be on location, lifting heavy equipment on my own. And the symptoms of PTSD, which manifested suddenly and unpredictably, as well as the need to be available to cooperate with the ongoing investigation, had made it unfeasible to do my job. Nevertheless, I still needed money to live on.

But the thing I wanted most was to know "the truth."

The truth—the facts—these things could not be distorted by money or time.

The lawyer and I were on different paths, and the meeting came to an end. I returned to MPD in the police car.

Fear of Coming Face-to-Face with Mr. Yamaguchi

Knowing that Mr. Yamaguchi had returned to Japan and gone back to work at TBS as if nothing had happened exerted tremendous emotional weight upon me. TBS was in a building on the same premises as Reuters, where I had my internship, and the fear that I might bump into him made going to work harrowing for me. Prior to the incident, I had always looked forward to going to the office, never knowing what story I would end up following that day, but now that workplace represented something totally different.

Over and over, I played out the scenario of what I would do if I saw him in my mind. I certainly didn't want to run away. I had no reason to flee. But the thought of not knowing the best way to react filled me with dread.

At lunchtime in particular, I became incapable of stepping foot outside of the building. As before, even catching sight of someone who resembled Mr. Yamaguchi triggered nausea and panic. As a result of this stress, I even fainted while on the phone at work, something that had never happened to me before. I came back to my senses with a start to the sound of my colleague on the other end of the line calling my name over and over again.

It was just as Mr. A. had told me in the beginning— maybe I wouldn't be able to continue working in this industry in Japan. I was starting to believe that. I was afraid of moving in the same circles as Mr. Yamaguchi and didn't want to pretend that I'd be able to go on as usual. His retaliation for my having gone to the police could happen at any given moment. I was scared he might be watching for my next move, that he might pressure me. Someone had given the word and the arrest warrant had been called off. They could have the means to pull strings that went beyond even my wildest imagination.

Emotionally, I felt more cornered than ever.

I received a call one night from a number I didn't recognize.

Nervous about who might be calling, I hesitated to answer, but then, thinking it might be a source, I mustered up the courage to pick up. It was Mr. A.

He had a new phone number, he told me, after being transferred from the Takanawa Police Department. I hadn't heard his voice since the day when he had been unable to arrest Mr. Yamaguchi.

As a member of the police force, it wouldn't have been right for him to contact me. But what he said was "It wasn't because I botched things up, that's all I wanted you to know." Mr. A. had been very professional—he had done his utmost for the investigation of my case. It pained him that I might think Mr. Yamaguchi hadn't been arrested because of a mistake he made. He also worried about the situation I was in.

I took this opportunity to attempt to confirm with Mr. A. when it was that First Investigation had learned of the arrest warrant.

Was it conceivable, with MPD as the supervising authority, that the day of arrest could have arrived without them ever receiving a report? In my case in particular, it turns out this would have been impossible. Previously Mr. A. had been explicit about the fact that he had been reporting back to what they referred to in-house as "headquarters"—MPD's First Investigation.

With a case that involved a person with social standing such as Mr. Yamaguchi, the local precinct wouldn't be making decisions on its own without reporting to First Investigation, so it follows that obtaining the arrest warrant would have entailed a similar reporting up. In addition, Mr. A. assured me that Prosecutor M., with whom he'd consulted in detail throughout the case, was a high-ranking, experienced person within the Public Prosecutor's Office "who was never wrong."

As a result of the arrest warrant not being carried out, now I, the victim, had to work in a building on the same premises as the suspect. Surely I had the right to ask about the warrant.

It was true, Mr. A. said, that prior to obtaining the arrest warrant, he had been sending detailed reports via the top brass at Takanawa Police Department to "headquarters." And, of course, that included when he reached the stage of applying for an arrest warrant.

"He's famous so he won't flee" had been the reason given for why the arrest was called off, so it should have stopped there—but that did not jive with First Investigation's explanation.

On that day, when Mr. A. had told me, "The stop order came from MPD, from the top," I had been led to believe that the sudden halt had come down on the day of the arrest, from somewhere even higher up than First Investigation.

But uncovering who exactly had given the stop order was not a simple thing. At the time, I didn't think I'd ever find out.

Reassuring Allies Appear

I conveyed to Mr. A. that I was desperate to know why the arrest warrant had not been executed, and whether it was still in effect. I wanted to do everything in my power to find out. I was willing to try any means. Doing so would help to clarify where the problems in this case originated.

Mr. A.'s response was similar to my uncle's. "I don't understand it myself, why the warrant wasn't executed. You're the victim, headquarters owe you a proper explanation. But if you ask them on your own, you won't get an accurate answer, so make sure you go there with a lawyer."

I felt that there was a huge wall before me, and it would be difficult to keep shouting so I might be heard on the other side. I was just one individual victim, up against a massive institution.

But, within that institution, there was someone in his right mind. And that person, who knew this case better than anyone, was telling me that I ought to keep speaking out.

In that moment—overwhelmed by a sense of my own powerlessness and crushed by the feeling that there wasn't anything else that I could do—Mr. A.'s words were a balm. I realized that I wasn't locked in a battle against the institution itself.

My opponent was somewhere in one of the higher

echelons. The investigator who served that institution was not at fault.

Mr. A. made it clear that he didn't want to criticize the police. Even as a member of the force, his moral fiber was never in question. It occurred to me how much courage it must have required for him to share these things with me.

But, if a single word from a higher-up could overrule the determination of the court, making it so that the arrest wasn't carried out and the investigation was cast into darkness, then this breakdown needed to be fully addressed. If the authorities conducting the investigation weren't functioning properly, then who or what were we ordinary citizens supposed to believe in? How were we expected to go about our lives? This also worried Mr. A.

Confirming the status of the arrest warrant was a battle against time. I didn't have a clear sense of the situation, but I needed to find out what I could while the warrant was presumably still valid.

The problem was whether or not I could find a lawyer I could trust—one who would be willing to deal with this matter with me. For a lawyer, there wasn't much of an advantage to confronting MPD.

Having resolved to find a lawyer on my own, I contacted the Tokyo 3 Bar Association's telephone counseling service, which offered consultation for victims of crimes, and a lawyer named Yoko Nishihiro took my call. She requested that we meet right away to discuss things in person.

Around the same time, the colleague at Reuters who, after I told her about my experience, had begun reporting about the "second rape," also gave me the name of Tomoko Murata, a lawyer whom she had met through her reporting and who specialized in sex crimes. "Give her a call," my colleague said.

Since I had just retained Ms. Nishihiro, I called Ms. Murata out of courtesy to explain that I had found someone else. It turned out that the two of them had known each other a long time and had worked together to represent women who had been involved in sex crime cases. The two of them agreed:

"It's definitely strange that the stop order came down so suddenly, just as they were on scene and about to arrest Mr. Yamaguchi. Ask anyone—another lawyer or someone who knows the workings of MPD—and they will all say that they've never heard of such a thing. It's better if we go to the police as a team."

And so they agreed to take on my case together.

Ms. Nishihiro told me later that, when she first heard my story, she thought to herself with surprise, *This really happens? It's like something you see on a TV drama!*

After what Mr. A. had told me, I felt an enormous boost to have these two lawyers tackling the case, with their keen awareness of the issues.

A few days later, they both accompanied me to MPD in order to ask the investigators about the arrest warrant. Previously, I had always been alone when passing through the strict security at the doors to this institution, but this time the two lawyers were with me. Whereas before, I always felt discouraged when I came here, now I was reassured.

The MPD investigators had the same things to say as last time, but there was one new update about the arrest warrant.

"Last week we sent back the arrest warrant. We have no further plans to apply for a new one."

I didn't understand at the time, but this was the first time MPD had given me a straight answer. It gave me a sense of closure.

We also learned that the arrest warrant had been in effect for a long time after all.

Mr. Yamaguchi's lawyer contacted Ms. Nishihiro and Ms. Murata several times after that. He wanted to know if I had changed my mind about taking an out-of-court settlement.

Submitting to the Prosecutor's Office
and the Ruling to Dismiss

On August 26, 2015, the case was submitted to the Public Prosecutor's Office.

In the month after the assault, I had drifted between staying at my friend K.'s house and at my parents', doing my utmost to avoid being by myself.

I ultimately decided to move. I had spoken to Mr. Yamaguchi about the area where I had been living at the time, and was uncomfortable on the off chance that he might know where it was. I had settled into that apartment after returning from New York and was moving out less than six months later—I didn't have any particularly attachment to the place anyway. I hoped that, by moving, I could leave behind the fearful memories and sleepless nights I had experienced there.

In October I met with Prosecutor K., who was now in charge of my case. That day, I again answered questions about the assault—I had lost count of how many times I had done this.

I told Prosecutor K. about how, when the police had stopped the arrest, I had tried contacting Prosecutor M. from Germany to find out what had happened, but I had been told that he had been taken off the case.

His response was to say that, because the case had been transferred from Prosecutor M. to him afterward, he hadn't been aware that I had called from Germany. Had he known, Prosecutor K. said, he would have explained things.

Then he added, "If the arrest being stopped was troubling for you or caused you to have doubts about how the police and the prosecutors were doing their jobs, then I apologize. You've already been traumatized enough by this incident—to have burdened you further was unnecessary, and the investigators ought not to have revealed it to you in the first place."

Did he mean to say that the fact that Mr. A. told me, the victim, that Mr. Yamaguchi had not been arrested was "unnecessary" and "ought not to have been revealed"? As far as I was concerned, the fact that the arrest had been stopped without any explanation at all was far worse. It seemed that the victim's right to know did not matter in the slightest.

Prosecutor K. subsequently questioned Mr. Yamaguchi in January 2016.

Approximately four months after the prosecutor's questioning took place, on May 30, 2016, Mr. Yamaguchi quit his job at TBS. One month later, Gentosha published a book he had written about Prime Minister Shinzo Abe, entitled *Sori* ("Prime Minister"), and he was then ubiquitous on television, often appearing as a commentator. Or so my friends told me.

I didn't have a TV in my new apartment. As much as possible, I tried to avoid seeing his face.

The life that Mr. Yamaguchi was leading now had nothing to do with me. The only thing I wished for was that the Japanese legal system would function properly.

Since the sight of his face would trigger a panic attack, I did what I could to prevent that from happening.

But one day, I found myself killing time in a bookstore. His book, *Sori*, displayed face up on a low shelf, caught my eye. Just seeing his name on the cover, my whole body went rigid.

A mere glimpse of his name or the sound of his voice was enough to overwhelm me all over again—my body remembered the fear, which then slipped easily into my reality. Memories wreaked so much havoc.

The second time I met with Prosecutor K. was mid-July 2016. No new developments came of our discussion. The prosecutor concluded with these remarks:

"I think that Mr. Yamaguchi was really wrong to have done what he did. Besides being married, he used his considerable standing and place within the system to underhandedly take advantage of your aspirations. That alone merits enough damage—his actions are absolutely inexcusable.

"Your email exchange put him on the defensive and he has retained a lawyer. From the prosecution's side, he could be convicted but, to be frank, it's difficult with the evidence we have. He's a deplorable man. He's habituated to this behavior—I can't help but think he's done this to others."

And then the prosecutor expounded at length on the

contradiction that existed within current Japanese law, in which quasi-rape was indeed a crime but it was actually quite difficult to put suspects on trial.

He began by speaking about the judiciary system:

"In Japan, sex crimes are very difficult to prove. Japanese criminal law tends to place tremendous subjectivity upon the suspect. And of course, since it's rare for the suspect to admit to the crime, they say that it was 'consensual.'

"Criminal law in the United States, though, allows for prosecution based on objective facts rather than on subjective accounts. In Japan, even when the suspect's guilt is clear, objective circumstances on their own are not enough for a conviction unless there is an admission of guilt.

"Powerful evidence is required. For instance, pictures or audio documenting the crime, or a third-party eyewitness. Something along those lines. I happen to have experience working with the American judicial system as well, so I'm familiar with both."

At the time, I didn't question his explanation—that it was difficult to apply the law against "quasi-rape" without an eyewitness who was at the scene, or without video of the crime. I simply accepted it. The larger problem, apparently, was the law itself. The crime of quasi-rape seemed unenforceable within Japanese law.

When I think about it now, though, one of the reasons why the arrest warrant had been issued in the first place was because of the possibility that the assault had been recorded on Mr. Yamaguchi's computer. And yet, it had been the police's decision not to execute the warrant.

When the case had been transferred from the Takanawa

Police Department to MPD's First Investigation, I was told that a domiciliary search of Mr. Yamaguchi's home had been conducted. Based on information I obtained myself, MPD had placed a call to TBS's Washington bureau—Mr. Yamaguchi's former workplace—several days before the home search.

And the search was residential, meaning that they only investigated his home and not his place of business.

This is how Mr. Yamaguchi described it in a 2016 Facebook post:

"I think it was in mid-May, officers from MPD arrived at my home and I learned for the first time that a criminal complaint had been filed against me. The two officers from MPD were extremely polite as I was informed that they requested my cooperation in a voluntary investigation."

A domiciliary search, like an arrest, requires a warrant to be enforced. What did he mean by a "voluntary investigation"? The police had explained to me that a domiciliary search had been conducted; they certainly hadn't described it as voluntary.

And MPD made no attempt to restore the data that may have been deleted from the computer. This task requires a specialist, and also costs time and money. But I never received any such explanation about it, nor did I ever see it documented anywhere. There was, however, no way for me to have known any of this at the time.

Prosecutor K. said this to console me:

"My predecessor was the one who handled this. If the victim is abroad and has been told that the arrest will take place, they are requested to return to Japan—I'm sure that you made preparations to fly home. To then be told that, in fact, we didn't arrest him, and there's no need to come back to Japan—this shouldn't happen.

"If the victim is informed, it's my opinion that the arrest must be carried out. This is a terrible shame; it absolutely should not have happened."

He concluded by saying, "I'm truly sorry."

On July 22, 2016, the ruling to dismiss the case was announced. I was informed of this result by one of my lawyers, five days later.

7/27/16

Dear Shiori, (cc: Ms. Murata)

I hope you are well.

I received contact today from Prosecutor K. that the decision was made on July 22 that your case is nonprosecutable; that the case has been dismissed.

I would like to set up a meeting in the coming days to discuss things further. I wanted to convey this information to you as soon as possible.

Sincerely,
Yoko Nishihiro

It was what I had expected, yet still, seeing it come to pass, I was left with a vast sense of helplessness.

CHAPTER SIX
"QUASI-RAPE"

There is a book called *Missoula: Rape and the Justice System in a College Town*. Written by Jon Krakauer, the powerhouse author known for *Into the Wild* and *Into Thin Air*, it depicts accusations of rape by star football players at the University of Montana.

Krakauer writes that rape is the most underreported serious crime in the United States. The same could be said about Japan.

According to data compiled in 2013 by the United Nations Office on Drugs and Crime, the number of rapes by country, per 100,000 population, is as follows:

1. Sweden	58.5
3. United Kingdom (England and Wales)	36.4
5. United States	35.9
23. France	17.5
38. Germany	9.2
68. India	2.6
87. Japan	1.1

What is your reaction to these statistics?

The Highest Incidence of Rape Worldwide
Is in Sweden?

The reason why the rate of rape is so high in Sweden, compared to other countries, is because of the method that Sweden uses to calculate the number of occurrences. For example, when a victim has been sexually abused by a relative over a long period of time, that doesn't count as a single incident; each time the victim was raped counts as a separate incident.

In addition, the environment there is much more conducive to filing criminal complaints. In 2015, women made up 31 percent of the Swedish police force. This includes not only officers in the field but also those in managerial positions.

In contrast, according to MPD statistics, women make up only 8.1 percent of the total number of Japanese police officers. This means that, as was my experience, a female victim who reports an assault will be surrounded by men throughout the process—from the investigators to the higher-ups who make decisions in her case.

And, since these figures were based on rapes that were reported to the police, they of course differ from the number of actual occurrences. The rate is 2.6 in India, where rape is known to be a severe problem. In other words, it's not that the incidence of rape is low—rather, what appears to be rare is the reporting of rape.

In the United States, where Krakauer wrote that rape is the most underreported serious crime, the number is 35.8.

Looking at these data, one sees that in Japan, as in India, the number of rapes *reported* is extremely low.

In a survey on violence between men and women conducted in 2015 by the Gender Equality Bureau of the Cabinet Office in Japan, one in fifteen women responded that they had "been forced to have intercourse by a member of the opposite sex."

Data in the United States indicate that one in five women say they have been a victim of rape. These numbers are not only reflective of differences in rates of incidence but they also point to different ways of defining rape.

Before the 2017 amendment to Japan's criminal law, Article 177 defined rape as "illicit sexual intercourse with a female," but the new language ("forced sexual intercourse") enables the inclusion of forced anal and oral sex. The statistic of one in five American women included both anal and oral sex, and with this revised language, the number of victims in Japan can be expected to grow.

I wanted to know more about the conditions in Sweden, where reporting for rape was much more common, so I visited the emergency rape center in Stockholm's Södersjukhuset Hospital.

The department there treats rape victims twenty-four hours a day, 365 days a year. The building looks like a typical general hospital from the outside, but the rape emergency center has two dedicated entrances. One of these bypasses the main waiting room, enabling someone to reach the reception desk without having to see anyone else. The interior rooms are partitioned into smaller areas to protect one's privacy, and though one can't be admitted for extended care, there is space to lie down and rest.

Also, a rape kit forensic exam can be performed up to

ten days after the assault has taken place, and the results are stored for six months. At the emergency center, the exam and treatment are administered to victims first, then they can receive counseling, and after, they can consider whether or not to file a police report.

Of course, when it comes to obtaining testimony and the other components necessary for court, the sooner a decision is made the better, but in the immediate aftermath of an assault, when one is suffering from both physical and emotional trauma, it can be a tremendous burden to have to reach a decision. By virtue of this system, those who have been assaulted can be saved from blaming themselves for not going to the police immediately, and from the blame of those around them who can't understand why they didn't file a criminal complaint right away, and from the indifference of those very authorities who say, as a result, there's nothing they can do.

Parenthetically, the proportion of those who file a report with the police within the six-month retention period after the results are received is 58 percent. The other 42 percent decide not to file a report for various reasons, including "I just want to forget all about it," "I was ashamed," and "I was afraid of appearing in court and facing my attacker."

Each person will have their own individual reaction to and way of facing the emotional and physical injuries they've sustained. Whatever they ultimately decide to do, it is thanks to the existence of a center like this that a system is in place where they can first receive treatment in a neutral environment—without being labeled as "victims"—and this is of vital importance.

And the same Södersjukhuset Hospital made headlines in 2015 when they established the world's first all-male rape crisis center. The center also treats transgender victims of assault.

The main center saw a total of 717 patients in 2016 (those under the age of thirteen were often directed to pediatric services, so the actual count may in fact be slightly larger). Among those, men still numbered only thirty-eight, but because the male rape crisis center offers specialized all-male counseling, they aim to treat more patients in the future.

A system such as this remains far from becoming a reality in Japan. However, centers that will take in such patients do exist, as I learned when I interviewed Dr. Chieko Nagai, the director of the Nirenoki Clinic in Tokyo. I'll return to this again later, but Dr. Nagai has done research on date-rape drugs.

She explained how the memory loss caused by date-rape drugs usually leads to victims' confusion, and even as it takes time for them to fully grasp the situation they now find themselves in, they tend to blame themselves for not being able to remember. But, she told me, this state of confusion is perfectly normal and, rather than blame themselves, they ought to be able to seek medical attention at a facility where a rape kit and blood tests can be administered.

The mistake I had made was going to a gynecologist's office first. Those kinds of general practitioners seldom have rape kits on hand—in order to be examined for rape and for drugs, I would have needed to go to an emergency room, Dr. Nagai said.

In the case of forced sexual intercourse, go to an emergency room. When you don't know what's best and can't decide, it is this choice that will determine your fate. For patients in the immediate aftermath of this experience, it's imperative that they be treated by medical professionals who understand that they require special consideration. I hope that Japan will soon have its own rape emergency center like the one at Stockholm's Södersjukhuset Hospital.

The "Consent Wall"

In the case of rape, the two main points of contention are generally:

1. Was there sexual intercourse?
2. Was there consent?

In my case, because there was no exam right after the attack, I was told repeatedly, "We cannot confirm whether sperm or injury was present," but even Mr. Yamaguchi didn't deny that sexual intercourse occurred. Of course it would have been preferable to have gotten an exam, but even still, that would have only been able to prove point number one.

The problem is proving number two.

For cases in which a victim is suddenly attacked on the street by a stranger and raped, it's rare for consent to be called into question. But, as mentioned earlier in this book, the vast majority of rape crimes involve victims who know their assailant.

How to proceed, then, in this case? If the suspect says, "She happily went along. It was consensual," then disproving that is no easy task. Even when the evidence clearly demonstrates that sexual intercourse took place, there are times where the police have dismissed the case, claiming that being in a room together constitutes consent.

In my case, the hotel security video plainly shows that I was dragged through the lobby, but after that, a certain amount of time elapsed while I was in Mr. Yamaguchi's hotel room.

During that period, was there consent or not?

It was pointed out to me repeatedly that a third party can't know what occurs behind closed doors. The public prosecutor referred to this as a "black box."

But how can someone who has been dragged, unconscious, into a room then give consent? If the law requires extensive evidence showing consent was not given in a case like mine, then it seems to me it's the law that is absurd.

There are some stunning precedents for such judgments regarding whether or not "consent" could be established.

For example, a high school senior who aspired to be a professional golfer was raped by her coach, a middle-aged man. The man ran a youth golf academy and had been coaching the girl since she was in her last year of middle school—he had become close with her family.

Under his strict tutelage, the girl's skills improved, and she progressed to the point of trying to go pro. Apparently the coach had a volatile personality—he subjected his own son to severe trainings that included corporal punishment in front of the girl; he got into arguments with the advisor to the golf team at the girl's school; when the advisor wasn't around he called him names; he made the girl cut her bangs, saying that they got in the way of playing golf; he became furious when she wore earrings or when she got a boyfriend, and made her stop both those things.

The coach was thirty-eight years older than the girl. When she was on tour, the two of them had meetings late at night in hotels, and there had been times when they took naps in his RV, but up until the attack, his actions had never strayed beyond that of a coach.

The coach always lectured the girl, accusing her of not having any grit, saying that the reason why she lost was because she was mentally weak. On the day of the attack, the coach called the girl at home and invited her to a golf training center, and came to pick her up in his car, but then he headed in the opposite direction of the training center.

He instead took her to a love hotel, saying, "I brought you here so you could learn how to have grit." He lectured her about golf for about half an hour, and then he raped her. The girl was rigid with shock and confusion.

I intentionally used the word "rape" to refer to this incident, but what do people think when they read this? The instructor whom she trusted, from whom she had been taking lessons for a long time, took her out on the pretext of practice and, using the excuse of it being related to her golf lessons, brought her to a hotel.

Surely she never imagined that he would end up doing such a thing to her. Or maybe she didn't want to believe it. She had never disobeyed her coach before, so perhaps she lay there petrified, not knowing how to express any sort of refusal to him, unable to accept that this was really happening to her?

The defendant, however, was acquitted of the charges.

Paralyzed and Unable to Resist

According to a survey from the rape center in Stockholm, 70 percent of rape victims report that, in the midst of the assault, they became unable to move or to resist, experiencing a dissociative state. This condition is called "tonic immobility," an involuntary state of paralysis—like playing dead—that animals enter into when they sense danger.

What is often called into question during rape trials in Japan is never whether the victim truly refused or not, but rather whether refusal was "clearly conveyed" to the suspect.

As for the reason why the girl didn't "clearly" refuse her coach, she testified that in addition to the mental confusion she experienced, "I was afraid that if I refused him, he wouldn't train me in golf anymore, or he would say terrible things about me to everyone. I thought it was better just to suffer through it."

And yet, the ruling gave no consideration to the kind of psychological coercion that was exerted.

To put it in extreme terms, if the suspect were to say, "I didn't realize that she was unwilling," it would potentially be enough—from a legal standpoint—to establish that there was consent.

This is known as the "consent wall." It should be noted that, in a rape crime, the question of whether or not the victim "said no" only comes up for those who are thirteen years of age or older; when the victim is under thirteen, the suspect is charged regardless.

When the attack occurs behind closed doors, proving what happened is no simple task.

The defendant can easily insist that there was consent when the other person was unconscious or doesn't remember, even more so when the crime was committed without any other witnesses. In these circumstances, the victim is unable to provide a definitive account that they did not give consent. These types of cases are considered "quasi-rape."

With no connection to sentencing, this nominal differentiation between rape and quasi-rape may be unique to Japan. True to form, the "quasi" prefix sets apart the definition of the term, designating it as not the thing itself but something similar or close to it—to a certain extent, that is.

But when I describe the Japanese terminology to English speakers, they are dumbfounded. "There is no such thing as 'sort-of' rape. Rape is rape."

Cases Involving Date-Rape Drugs

It often happens that cases of "quasi-rape" involve alcohol or date-rape drugs.

However, very few people in Japan are aware of the existence of date-rape drugs. Even though sleeping pills are frequently used in rape crimes, the public is still not generally aware of the danger.

In my case, when I spoke to my friend S. two days after the attack, I was under the impression that a single dose of this kind of substance took less than twenty-four hours to leave your system.

But it turns out that, according to the aforementioned Dr. Nagai, although it's difficult for a general medical practice to do so, there are specialized labs where it's possible to process urine tests that can detect substances even more than two days later. Although the time period for drug excretion will vary from person to person and by substance, she said that a blood test could detect substances even a week later.

Dr. Nagai's research began after treating a patient named M. She had gone out for drinks after work with a female colleague and two male superiors. When she regained consciousness, she was in a hotel, naked, being assaulted by the two men, she said. M. has a high tolerance for alcohol, and hadn't had so much to drink that she would have blacked out, and yet she had no memory of what had happened.

Dr. Nagai took this opportunity to delve into the literature available in the United States and Japan in order to gain a deeper understanding of date-rape drugs. Her reading led her to informational materials from the Rape Treatment Center (RTC) at the UCLA Santa Monica Medical Center, published in 2000 in the *National Institute of Justice Journal*. In particular, the column "Learning from Victims" by Gail Abarbanel caught her attention. Here are a few excerpts:

> Victims were in what seemed like a comfortable social environment, such as a restaurant, party, or club. Unbeknownst to them, someone slipped a drug into their drink. As they consumed the drink, they began to feel disoriented or sick. The next thing they remembered was waking up hours later, sometimes in a different location.
>
> When they regained consciousness, some victims were unsure if they had been sexually assaulted. Others found signs that they had been: they were undressed; they had semen stains on their bodies and/or clothing;

they had vaginal or anal trauma, such as soreness and/ or lacerations. All of these victims reported significant memory impairment. Most could not recall what was done to them, who participated, or how many people were present while they were unconscious. Some could remember brief, intermittent periods of awakening, during which they were aware of their surroundings but were unable to move or speak. . . .

When victims began to report these crimes to the authorities, their cases often were dismissed. One victim was told, "He has his memory, you don't have yours. There's no evidence. The case is closed."

In many instances, crucial physical evidence was never gathered from victims or crime scenes.

For Dr. Nagai, these points summarized the issues involved with drug-facilitated rape.

Dr. Nagai's patient, M., was terrified to go back to work after the attack, which led to her dismissal. Based on M.'s testimony, Dr. Nagai believed it was likely that date-rape drugs had been used, and to support that conviction, she translated the RTC's materials into Japanese to demonstrate medical proof of M.'s condition. In a civil trial that lasted more than four years, M. eventually won her case.

During the trial, M. said that there were times when she agonized over whether to give up on prosecuting. She almost couldn't bear the slander and abuse directed by the defendants' lawyer not only toward herself but toward her family as well. But despite the PTSD, severe depression, and the acute emotional anguish of her experience, she persevered, knowing that if she gave up now, she'd spend the rest of her life in tears.

The drugs often used to facilitate rape are sleeping pills and tranquilizers commonly prescribed in hospitals and clinics. Whenever Dr. Nagai prescribes these to her patients, she always urges caution—approximately one out of a hundred people experience memory loss as a side effect.

For example, there have been cases in which people have woken up in the morning to find a half-eaten bento meal on the kitchen table that they don't remember consuming, or sent emails that they don't recall ever writing. From outside appearances, a person's behavior seems normal, but they have no memory of their actions at all.

When these drugs are used in conjunction with alcohol, this side effect is further enhanced.

Examples of Reports in Japan

In 2015, an article was published in Japan that attempted to offer a more detailed pharmacological assessment.

Entitled "Triazolam Impairs Avoidance Reaction—A Scientific Proof Why the Victim Does Not Escape from Drug-Facilitated Sexual Assaults," the article was authored by Keiko Shimizu, Tomohiro Ohmura, Katsuhiro Okuda, Masaru Asari, Hiroshi Shiono, and Kazuo Matsubara, and appeared in *Acta criminologiae et medicinae legalis Japonica*. (An English translation of this article was published in *Journal of Forensic Psychology* in 2016.) The contents are highly specialized and technical, but I will try to give a brief outline of the relevant points.

According to the article, crimes involving date-rape drugs have been increasing in Japan since the late 1990s. In one example, a fifty-three-year-old doctor and former medical school lecturer invited to his apartment seven young women in their twenties whom he had met at a beach resort. He gave them alcohol and fed them food that had been laced with sleeping pills, and proceeded to assault them while they were unable to resist.

The presiding judge's sentence offered harsh criticism: "A premeditated crime with a strong potential for re-offense, the suspect's depraved method inflicted serious damage upon the victims." (As it were, the reason they reached a guilty verdict was due to the number of victims, which broke down the wall of consent.)

The authors of the article cite a case from 1995 in which a rental video shop owner and an office worker coaxed a female high school student to a karaoke bar, where they gave her soda containing powdered sleeping pills. When she lost consciousness, they sexually assaulted her and recorded a video of the assault, with the intention of selling it on the black market.

The investigating authorities were unable to comprehend how the victim could have no recollection of the assault, so they made an inquiry to the authors' academic department concerning the pharmacological effects of the drugs. Using an experimental animal model, the authors were able to prove that, when combined with alcohol, this kind of drug induced a neuropharmacological mechanism of amnesia, in which the brain is unable to form memories of events.

These results were then used as reference materials in the trial. (The reason why these were admitted as evidence is likely due to the existence of the video that was shot for illegal sale, which proved the factual details.)

In the United States, governmental institutions have long been using the internet to warn the public about date-rape drugs. Currently, sites to raise awareness are maintained by public entities such as the Departments of Justice and Health and Human Services, the FBI, NIH, state governments, and educational institutions, as well as private-sector sites like Wikipedia and those which provide medical information.

It is extremely easy to obtain the sleeping pills and drugs that are used in these crimes. The pharmacological properties of these substances induce a soporific effect that causes drowsiness; an antianxiety effect that dulls a normal response to danger; and a muscle-relaxant effect that numbs and inhibits movement. In addition, it induces anterograde amnesia, which produces fragmented or total memory loss for a period after taking the drug.

There are ninety-five active ingredients included in 588 different brands of prescription drugs available in Japan for which the packaging lists anterograde amnesia as a side effect. Of the substances for which the likelihood of inducing anterograde amnesia is highest, even slightly exceeding the recommended dosage significantly increases the potential for it.

Cases of anterograde amnesia linked to these kinds of drugs were reported as early as the 1960s around the world. In one article, three neuroscientists described traveling to attend a conference. With the hope of preventing jet lag, they each took one of these drugs with alcohol while on the plane, and all three reported experiencing memory loss over the following ten hours.

One of the scientists was accompanied by his wife and they passed through immigration and customs, went sightseeing in the city, chatted over dinner, and spent the night in a hotel—and he had no memory of any of this. But to those who were with him at the time, he appeared perfectly normal.

Another of the scientists also passed through immigration and customs, changed planes, checked into a hotel, met up with his fellow researchers and had dinner with them, but he didn't remember a thing.

When the third scientist's flight landed, his baggage had not arrived with him, so after going through immigration and customs and exchanging money, he went to the airline's lost property office, only to find that a lost baggage claim form had already been submitted in his own handwriting. He did not recall filling it out.

There are examples of reports in Japan as well.

When a doctor who developed insomnia as a result of irregular shifts took a sleeping pill for the first time, he immediately went to sleep and, when he awoke the next morning, was perplexed by the thanks he received from a nurse who had been working the night shift. Apparently the hospital had asked him to make a house call in the middle of the night, and he had done so as per usual—though he had no memory of it.

The stupor induced by taking such drugs inhibits one's ability to avoid danger, and this state is even more likely to occur when consumed in conjunction with alcohol. There is significant memory loss when these drugs are combined with even a small amount of alcohol—much more than the memory loss that can occur from a blackout caused by heavy drinking alone.

A report from the US Department of Justice notes that there have been instances when metabolites from these kinds of drugs were detected in hair three weeks after taking them, and lists methods that can detect these traces even after some time has passed since an assault.

In light of the drug-facilitated rapes that have been on the rise in Japan since the 1990s, investigating authorities need to take initiative in devising effective testing systems like those in the United States, so that when a rape kit is administered to victims in a medical facility, blood, urine, and hair tests can also be taken right away. In the confused state immediately following an assault, it's difficult to think these things through, but if information was more readily available and systems were already in place, this process wouldn't be as unmanageable. And not just for the sake of yourself, but also with the hope of being able to advise your friends, should they ever experience something like this.

Cases That Broke Down the "Consent Wall"

Let's set aside date-rape drugs for the time being and consider the legal conditions that would need to align in order to break down the "consent wall" in crimes of quasi-rape in Japan. I searched for cases in which a guilty verdict was issued, and here is what I learned.

A famous judoka was found guilty of quasi-rape in Tokyo District Court, having assaulted a first-year university student who was a pupil of his. The attack occurred at a training camp for the university's judo team, so there were several witnesses.

The defendant and several members of the team, including the coach—seven people in all—had gone to a yakitori restaurant. The defendant had made a rule that anyone who raised their glass had to drain it, and in this way had gotten the victim heavily intoxicated. Later when the group moved on to a karaoke bar, the victim passed out. After, the defendant carried her on his back and returned to the hotel where they were staying. He went to the victim's room, where he raped her on the bed while she was unconscious.

The victim came to in the middle of the assault, and although she tried to resist, he was stronger and she was unable to push him off.

One of the main reasons why the defendant was found guilty is that he lied in his deposition. He stated that, while they were at the karaoke bar, the victim had repeatedly made advances toward him, but as all the other team members had seen, she had been inebriated and passed out.

When one of the other judo team members came looking for the judoka and knocked on the hotel room door while the assault was taking place, the defendant pressured the victim to answer and say that he wasn't there. In court, the defense used this to assert that the crime "didn't match up with quasi-rape."

But the ruling recognized that "amid her panic and confusion at this sudden sexual abuse from her judo instructor, whom she respected, it is entirely plausible that she would have been unable to know how to react in the moment and that she would have gone along with and obeyed the defendant."

The explanation went on to say that, in contrast with a situation in which the victim is attacked by a complete stranger, the fact that she knew the defendant may well have led to her feeling ashamed when her teammate came to the door, and could explain why she didn't ask for help.

This is of course perfectly reasonable—but then I wonder why, in the case against the golf instructor, the same mental state wasn't acknowledged for that victim.

In Japan, an assault is considered rape when there is violence or a threat to a "degree that is markedly difficult to resist." That is to say, if the victim can't prove that it was difficult to resist the violence or threats of her attacker, then usually the defendant will be found not guilty. It's very common within the context of relationships between students and their coaches for psychological threats to go unrecognized.

The burden of providing evidence of violence or threats is one of the key amendments that needed to be made to Japan's criminal code. Otherwise, it suggests that if there's no evidence that a victim struggled to a reasonable extent, then the crime is pardonable. We mustn't forget the results of the survey in which 70 percent of those who experienced sexual violence reported the condition of tonic immobility, being unable to move.

When the former criminal code was written a hundred and ten years ago, Japanese society was wholly patriarchal.

A woman's right to express herself was not publicly recognized. In that era, not even all men had the right to vote. It is patently ridiculous for laws reflecting the spirit of that time to be applied to court cases today.

And yet, when the criminal law was amended in 2017, this point was unfortunately not revised. If a parent or guardian is charged with committing rape or an obscene act with a child under the age of eighteen, it falls under "sexual acts by a guardian" or "obscene conduct by a guardian," but coaching is not included in such relationships.

In future rape cases, victims over the age of thirteen will still be required to prove the existence of violence or threats. Especially in cases of quasi-rape, the wall of consent will remain, towering higher than ever.

A review of the amendment's measures and implementation is set to take place three years from the time of this writing, in 2020. We must take this opportunity to lessen the burden of proof for violence and threats. Because even when neither are noticeably present, there are situations in which sex is forced upon the victim, as in the case of the golf instructor and student.

Society needs to educate and spread awareness that, instead of "If I don't say NO, then I don't mean NO," the fact is that "If I don't say YES, then I don't consent."

With the amendment, victims are no longer required to file a complaint. So even if the victim doesn't press charges, the suspect can still be indicted. This, however, is meaningless until the investigation process and the court procedures that constitute a harrowing "second rape" for the victim are reformed.

If we are to change the status quo, one in which more women prefer not to report rape, it will require significantly more reform to the justice system.

CHAPTER SEVEN

CHALLENGES

Let's return to my case. All the serious problems within the Japanese legal system with regard to sex crimes aside, why had the arrest been called off that day?

When I spoke to Mr. A., I asked him candidly, "Is it a problem within the police force?"

"I'm afraid it is," he replied, "but there's no definitive proof."

On the day of the intended arrest, Mr. A. had told me, "The stop order came from MPD, from the top." First and Second Investigation are both part of and report to the chief of Criminal Investigation. In the fall of 2015, it was suggested to me by a journalist that this "top" must refer to the chief of Criminal Investigation.

At that time, the post was held by Itaru Nakamura. According to Mr. A., on the day of the arrest, all of the materials from the investigation had been gathered at the Takanawa Police Department in preparation for the questioning that was to follow. So then what exactly did Mr. Nakamura see that made him decide to stop the arrest?

And if the decision that was applied on the scene at the airport was indeed manipulated from above, what did Mr. A. think of it?

When I asked him at the time, his response had been that he had always hoped to avoid finding himself in such a situation.

"You've been pressured before?" I asked.

"Yes."

Mr. A. went on to say that previously, though, it had only ever been pressure. Such a blatant intervention had never happened before—an arrest suddenly being canceled on the same day it was to be carried out.

Kiyoshi Shimizu's Book

Being a journalist, I had naturally considered going to the press to make my case known, or penning an article myself about the problems I'd encountered. This idea first came to me when the arrest warrant wasn't carried out. I feared that remaining silent would allow the investigation to be distorted. And I wanted as many people as possible to know these controversial issues about quasi-rape.

I consulted with my boss at Reuters.

I had confided in him early on about the assault. He had asked me how much time I was taking off, and I wasn't going to be able to keep making the excuse that it was all treatment for my knee. I also told a close colleague who had been worried about me. I hated lying about why I couldn't come to work.

When Mr. Yamaguchi's arrest was called off so suddenly, I suggested to Reuters that they investigate the matter. Several colleagues expressed keen interest in the idea.

However, when it was discussed during a meeting, the bureau chief said they wouldn't be able to feature the story. The reason, he said, was that they wouldn't be able to report on it objectively because the victim was one of their own employees.

Also, as Reuters primarily distributed news to international media, there wasn't demand for this kind of domestic Japanese news. And the evidence was all in the hands of the police, which definitely would have presented a problem.

So then, who would report on the story?

Since the story's newsworthiness was in question, it was necessary to have facts that could speak to some specific point. I needed to find one way or another to shift the course of the investigation as quickly as possible.

An opportunity soon presented itself. MPD finally decided to send the documents from the case file to the Public Prosecutor's Office. I couldn't miss this chance. It was at this time that I decided to use my connections to try to reach out to Kiyoshi Shimizu, a journalist who was renowned for scooping police and prosecutors' investigations, notably in the Okegawa stalker-murder and the Ashikaga murder cases.

One day, visiting a friend—this was before I found out about the arrest warrant—I was in her foyer, tying my shoelaces, when my eye fell upon a book on the shelf by the door, *The Murderer Is Out There* by Kiyoshi Shimizu, published in 2013.

"What is this? That's quite a title!" I said.

"Ah! I meant to lend that to you—you have to read it, Shiori. Take it with you for the flight to Germany," she said, handing me the book.

It was as if this encounter was destined to happen, because reading Mr. Shimizu's book had a profound effect on me.

Beginning in 1979, a series of kidnappings and murders of little girls took place within a six-mile radius along the border between Tochigi and Gunma prefectures. All five cases involving these children were similar, but only one was solved and became known as the "Ashikaga murder."

The man who was arrested for the murder had been convicted and was serving time in prison, while the other four cases remained unsolved. Another man, who had been strongly suspected of being connected to the crimes, had never been arrested and was living freely.

What if that man was the murderer? Could the one who was currently in prison have been falsely accused?

The fact was, the imprisoned man had always claimed to be innocent.

With awe-inspiring investigative ability, Mr. Shimizu would go on to expose not only how the police's investigation was filled with deception, but also the cover-up that ensued to protect the organization. Mr. Shimizu's investigation led to a retrial for Toshikazu Sugaya, the man who had been convicted and imprisoned, and he was later acquitted.

What left the strongest impression on me at the time was Mr. Shimizu's acute insight regarding the judicial system, the victims, and the media. And the fundamental differences between the authorities, who want only to see someone arrested and tried, and the families of the victims, who wish to know the truth—not to mention the media that do nothing more than report the "story" assembled by the police.

Though the mistakenly arrested Sugaya had given up on the police, who had extracted a false confession from him, he had held on to the vague hope for the appearance someday of a noble figure who would realize his innocence.

This passage from the book resonated with me:

Follow the mystery. Seek the facts. Keep going back to the scene. Find the people who are there. Make every effort to hear their stories. These may be the victims, they may be the families of victims. These are damaged souls. Their sensitivity is heightened. All the more so if they have been harassed by the press. What else is there to do but be present for these souls, listen to their murmuring voices, and convey what they have to say?

The angry voices of the powerful and entitled will resound without anyone's help. But not those murmurs. They don't reach the ears of the state or the general public. Indeed, the mission of a journalist is to act as their intermediary.

Mr. Shimizu never blamed the parents in the murder case, who had left their child alone in the car. Whatever the crime, whatever the accident, he always refrained from writing things off as "special circumstances for special people."

This book taught me about the police and prosecutor systems, and about the dynamics of these organizations. And the following lines would become a guiding principle for me to follow as a journalist: "Bend your ear to the quieter voices while questioning the louder ones. What to report on and for what purpose? I believe these are the questions you must always ask yourself."

At the time, Kiyoshi Shimizu was working for Nippon TV. I'd once had an internship at the New York branch of NTV; I still thought highly of them and felt I could trust their standing in the media.

An acquaintance gave me Mr. Shimizu's contact information, and when I reached out, he immediately offered to help. He thought I should speak to the reporters on the MPD beat, and he proceeded to introduce me to the journalists from NTV's kisha club at MPD, the exclusive association of reporters who covered police-related activities.

An Icy Reception from the Press

The NTV reporters on the MPD beat filmed an interview with me on the same day that I met them and told them my story. At first, they intended to run it to coincide with the documents from my case file being sent to the prosecutor. They wanted to look into why the arrest warrant hadn't been executed, and by timing it with the move to the prosecutor, it presented a chance to use the media to ask whether the investigation was being conducted legitimately.

But when the police sent the case file to the prosecutor, NTV didn't run the story.

I received word at the end of 2015 that "they want to do it at the beginning of the year." Yet this didn't happen either. Finally, I was told, "They'll run it if the case is dismissed." *So then what will their angle be?* I wondered. Frankly, I was leery. If they were waiting until the case resulted in dismissal, how would the truth ever come out? I had no idea.

This back-and-forth with NTV was exhausting.

I had done everything I could think of, and still this small window of opportunity had closed before my eyes. All that was left for me to do at that point was to await the prosecutor's decision. I had no other choice. My lawyers had sharply warned me that the wrong move could negatively impact the prosecutor's decision.

During my second interview with Prosecutor K., as I began to sense that the case was going to be dismissed, I realized how foolish I had been to take the NTV reporters at their word about when they would run the story.

When I thought this over more thoroughly, there was never any way it could have happened. If the case were dismissed, there would be a gag order. Instead of being able to call out the problems with my case, I would be forced to accept the fact of the dismissal—despite the actual facts. There was nothing else I could do except comply with it.

And, as expected, even after the case was dismissed, NTV still did not run the story.

Was there really no one in the mainstream media in Japan who would question the rulings of the judicial system?

Perhaps it was difficult for reporters on the MPD beat, as part of a larger corporation, to initiate their own stories. But if that were the case, I would rather they had said so honestly. I wish they had just told me why they couldn't run it instead of repeatedly postponing the story.

And still, each time I saw them, they asked me for more information without offering any explanation.

They had requested to meet my lawyers and had interviewed us together numerous times. Ultimately, up to when I finally held a press conference, the NTV reporters never once ran anything about the contents of these meetings, and at one point I even suspected they might be leaking the information I had given them or about my next steps to the authorities. I had similar concerns about Mr. A.

I no longer knew whom I could trust.

I had also met a reporter from *Tokyo Shimbun*. She had a reputation for being an excellent editorial writer and had listened empathetically to my story. But she too had told me that the timing was difficult for reporting on my case.

Others explained to me that, had Mr. Yamaguchi been arrested it would have made the news, but it was difficult to report on the fact that he had *not* been arrested.

Objectively, the evidence probably was insufficient to sustain a trial. And yet, in this case, Mr. Yamaguchi not being arrested is, in itself, the thing that is ludicrous. Wasn't this exactly what investigative journalism was all about?

Whatever one might say, in the end it is the media that dictate what merits reporting and what is newsworthy. And of course various circumstances factor into that equation—I understand that—but what confounded me was seeing the various doors of the investigative authorities, followed by those of the press, close one after another before my eyes.

When the case was deemed nonprosecutable in July of 2016 and its dismissal marked the end of the investigation, this decision didn't reflect the truth—it was a kind of gag order, an attempt to silence me.

Once that judgment came down, I put aside this particular reality for a time. I didn't want to think about it anymore. The investigation had lasted sixteen months and I was exhausted. And after everything, this was what had come of it. While I had been waging war against the Japanese legal system and its institutions, I'd had no other choice but to put aside my own trauma.

And yet, my efforts had been futile. The problems that plagued the Japanese legal system remained unresolved.

I couldn't bear to tell my friends and family right away about the dismissal. A year and four months had passed since the assault, and they no longer talked about it. They must have thought it would be better for me to do whatever I could to try to forget about it, not to keep dredging it back up. And I did my very best to behave normally in front of them.

Mary F. Calvert's Photography

I gradually continued to pick up freelance work.

But, if I kept making references to the attack, voicing my objections to the investigative systems and pushing for legal reform, it would likely be difficult to find work while living in Japan, even on a freelance basis and for clients abroad.

Around this time, my friend I. attended a conference for women in international business where Prime Minister Shinzo Abe was a guest speaker and various media types were present. In the hotel where the venue was, she saw someone who looked like Mr. Yamaguchi.

I. is a very close friend of mine who was helping me with the research for my case. Because she was so familiar with the details, when she saw this man she froze before immedi- — ately calling me. I, too, could easily have been reporting on this conference. It may or may not have actually been Mr. Yamaguchi, but by that point I had stopped working in the building adjacent to his, so there was no way to know where or when our paths might cross.

I was in this mindset when I had the opportunity to see a photography exhibit. Each year, the Tokyo Photographic Art Museum held an exhibition called World Press Photo. I had gone the previous year and had been blown away by how spectacularly a single image could manage to convey the life story of the photographic subject. I had looked forward to attending the exhibition again.

That year, my eyes were riveted by the first-prize photo in the "Long-Term Projects" category, taken by Mary F. Calvert.

This press photo was part of a series that followed incidents of rape and sexual assault prevalent in the US military. The mission of Calvert's long-term photojournalism project was to trace the scars of sexual assault by documenting the lives of survivors of military sexual trauma.

Considering how my own assault was disregarded by the media as something that "happens all the time," I hadn't expected to encounter the topic of rape at the World Press Photo exhibition.

The aftermath of sexual assault has a tremendous effect on a victim's life. Her suffering, and that of her family, is long term. Wounds that won't heal, drawn-out trials, homelessness as a result of the inability to go back to work, inescapable anguish that leads to suicide—these torments were painstakingly detailed in Calvert's photographs.

The one that left the strongest impression on me followed Carri Leigh Goodwin, who served in the US Marine Corps and was assaulted by her recruiter and also by a higher-ranking service member, and later died by suicide. The photo was of her diary, featuring a drawing of a slit wrist. I stood before it, mesmerized.

Alongside the drawing, Carri had written the words "IF ONLY IT WAS THIS EASY."

By "it" I assume she meant her bleeding wrist. Dying. Putting an end to her pain. Taking her own life.

Even now, the mere recollection of that drawing evokes for me the sense of being plunged into a deep and inescapable darkness. It's impossible for that vivid scar not to hit close to home.

Carri was bullied by her commander for reporting the assault, and then discharged for misconduct. Her father, Gary Noling, knew nothing about what had happened, and thought that Carri was coming home on leave. Five days after he picked her up at the bus station, Carri drank herself to death.

When her personal belongings were returned, Carri's diary was among them, and Gary learned why his daughter wanted to die. Toward the end of her diary, Carri had written, "Dad, there are some things I never told you that I should have," and she went on to explain what had happened to her.

Calvert's photograph of Gary standing alone in Carri's room, untouched since her death and with a large photo of

Carri visible, conveys with agonizing clarity the pain and suffering of the family left behind.

Rape occurs in every country, in every institution, in every organization. The perpetrator who holds authority is protected by their organization, and the facts are distorted. What happened to Carri is by no means uncommon.

To this day, I wonder just how many people have been forced to go on living, their hearts shattered.

And how many of them, like Carri, have taken their own lives?

After the attack, I myself had considered the same choice many times. I felt as though everything inside me had been obliterated.

However much I tried, however much I wanted to go back to being who I was before, it was impossible—all that was left was an empty husk of my former self.

But encountering these photographs reinforced the importance of what I had to say and caused me to reconsider. If I were going to die, there would be time for that later—after doing everything I could and using all that I had to confront the systemic problems that I knew needed to change.

Carri is no longer able to tell her own story. But she managed to leave a powerful message behind through the lens of a photojournalist. Standing before these photographs, I realized that I still had a voice of my own. There was no way I could let things end like this.

I would speak up and speak out. I had no other choice. My job was to bear witness. To remain silent would condone the crime that had been committed.

Petitioning the Committee for the
Inquest of the Prosecution

The only option left was to bring my case before the Committee for the Inquest of the Prosecution.

No matter the outcome, I knew I had to exhaust all possible options. I wanted to hold on to the last sliver of hope I had for Japanese society. And how could I speak to all the systemic problems if I didn't pursue every alternative?

The Committee for the Inquest of the Prosecution is set up to reconsider whether the public prosecutor's decision was appropriate, for situations where the victim feels that the dismissal of their case was unjust.

The inquest committee is made up of eleven eligible-to-vote citizens, chosen by lot, who review the documents that were presented in the case. Depending on the circumstances, they may hear an opinion from the prosecutor, or there may be questioning of the complainant or witnesses.

After deliberations, the inquest committee may decide to reverse the decision of the prosecutor, deeming it a "chargeable offense"; however, that requires the agreement of at least eight of the eleven members. Inquest decisions that concur with a case's dismissal, or alternatively decide that the dismissal was unjust (e.g., they decide the investigation was unsatisfactory and recommend that it be redone) require the agreement of at least six members.

Even when there's a "chargeable offense" decision, what comes next is not straightforward. The public prosecutor conducts a reinvestigation. They may decide that the case is prosecutable, but they also may decide to dismiss it again. In the latter situation, it is then sent back to the inquest committee, and if once again eight or more members deem the case to be prosecutable, there will be a "forcible indictment." This means that the trial will proceed without the assent of the public prosecutor.

After I decided to petition the Committee for the Inquest of the Prosecution, I filed a request for the disclosure of evidence in September 2016. This provides access to all of the evidence that the Public Prosecutor's Office has on hand for my case, which, as the victim, is within my rights.

I didn't expect much—I figured either they wouldn't release anything, or if they did release something, the documents would all be redacted and blacked out. But my lawyers were surprised when, several months later, they reviewed the disclosed materials. The prosecutor had released plenty of evidence in the case.

For my part, I too gathered as much evidence and testimony as possible. This would take time, but I was finally ready.

The Taxi Driver Confirms His Testimony

After the case was transferred to MPD from the Takanawa Police Department, it had been explained to me that they intended to meet with the taxi driver and other witnesses, in order to conduct a more thorough investigation.

It was still a mystery to me what they had revised in the report.

I located the taxi company and the driver who had driven Mr. Yamaguchi and me to the hotel, and I took a ride with him in his taxi to hear his version of the story.

"It was a striking experience, so I remember it well," the driver said about that night. I was surprised that, almost two years later, he still vividly recalled details about the two of us.

The taxi driver's version of events was consistent with what Mr. A. had told me at the time. Here is a detailed description of the driver's testimony.

After 11 p.m. on a Friday night about two years ago, I picked up a man and woman in my taxi, in the vicinity of the Ebisu-Minami intersection. The man wore a grayish suit; he had short hair, a beard, and wore glasses. The woman had on boyish clothing, pants and a blouse. They talked about how delicious the sushi had been, so I figured they may have dined at the fancy sushi bar that was near the Ebisu-Minami intersection. The woman had gotten in first, so she was on the right side, and the man sat on the left.

After they got into the taxi, when we were in the vicinity of the intersection at Ebisu-Minami Itchome, the woman said, "Please take me to a nearby train station." The nearest station was Ebisu, but that was back in the opposite direction, so I replied, "The closest station is Meguro." She replied, "Then please go to Meguro Station." During this time, the man didn't say anything.

In the taxi, the two of them seemed to be talking about work. From this, I deduced that they were professional acquaintances, rather than a couple.

When we were in the vicinity of the intersection in front of Kohsei General Hospital, the woman said, "Take me to Meguro Station, please." Again, the man didn't say anything.

As we neared the intersection with Meguro-Dori Avenue, I said, "We'll be there soon," and this time, the man spoke. "Go to the Miyako Hotel," he said. The woman said, "Please drop me off at the station first," but the man was saying something like, "We still have work matters to discuss, I won't do anything." Some time after that, the woman had gone quiet, but since I didn't turn around to look behind me, I don't know what state she was in.

I confirmed with the man that he wanted me to go to the hotel, and I headed toward the Sheraton Miyako Hotel. When I pulled into the covered entrance to the hotel, the man paid the fare and urged the woman to get out, but she didn't move at all.

It was Friday night—peak hours for fares—and I hoped they would get out quickly, so I turned around.

The man was not having much success pulling her toward the door, so he got out of the taxi and set his briefcase down, then put his shoulder under her arm and dragged the woman out of the car.

The woman entered the hotel, more or less being carried by the man. There was a hotel bellman, watching with concern.

After they got out, I pulled away from the hotel. A little while later, I noticed a smell—not the usual smell of vomit, it was more like vinegar mixed with liquor. *Not again*, I thought, and turned around to look in the back seat. On the side where the woman had been sitting, undigested food had been vomited up and left on the seat.

I brought the taxi back to the garage to be cleaned. Since it was already late, I called it a night.

Doubts about MPD's Investigation Report

Why did I need to collect this testimony myself?

I had learned that the investigation report compiled by MPD did not include the taxi driver's testimony that the "woman had repeatedly asked to be taken to a train station."

The officer from First Investigation had explained to me that they would be taking more detailed statements from the individuals involved who had already been questioned. The taxi driver's questioning by the Takanawa Police took place about one month before the case was transferred to First Investigation. So, by looking at the materials that were handed over, I assumed that when MPD had conducted their questioning, the driver's memory would have faded.

But that was not so.

Even after almost two years, he could still recall the details of that night with precision. Questioning the driver myself, I realized that—oddly—he had only ever spoken with investigators from the Takanawa Police Department. The driver had meticulously noted the dates in his calendar.

The first time the Takanawa Police Department had called the taxi company where he worked was on May 13, 2015. They asked him to come to the police box at Shinagawa Station, where he spoke with an investigator. The investigator who questioned him about the incident took notes. Several days later, the driver was called into the Takanawa Police Department, where he gave a formal statement.

The driver said that these were the only two times he was questioned by the police.

Which means that, after the case was transferred from the Takanawa Police Department to MPD, they never questioned him at all. So, what was the explanation I got from First Investigation that they would be questioning those involved all over again? Just what *was* in their report anyway?

The Idea for a Press Conference

On the same day that I petitioned the Committee for the Inquest of the Prosecution, I thought about going public with a press conference. But I didn't make up my mind right away. Just as first going to the police was a major decision, holding a press conference would require much more courage—like leaping over a chasm, or maybe more like jumping off a cliff.

At first, I considered appearing together with other victims of sexual crimes or with people from human rights groups.

It just so happened that, at the same time, I had been reporting on chikan—public groping or harassment that often occurs on public transportation in Japan—and I had been interviewing women who had experienced chikan or other forms of sexual assault. As a result of my research, I had met other rape victims and had listened to their stories.

This was when the amendment to the criminal law had been proposed in the Diet, and it seemed like the perfect time for calling attention to the systemic problems with crimes of rape and quasi-rape in Japan and, alongside other victims of sexual assault, for talking about the reform that needed to accompany revisions to the legal code.

I had discussed the idea with my parents, and they had given me their approval.

But although preparations were underway, when it came time to decide upon a date for the press conference, I was seized with various concerns.

Having just petitioned the Committee for the Inquest of the Prosecution, I knew my own case was not yet over. Holding a press conference could give rise to new problems. I had decided that if questions came up during the press conference that were related to individual circumstances, I would not avoid talking about my own experiences. After all, without such experience, how would I be able to speak to the specific need for reform?

But, if I were to mention Mr. Yamaguchi, would the conversation veer away from investigations and the legal system, and be treated simply as gossip? I had heard that, since Mr. Yamaguchi's demotion, he now had numerous right-leaning supporters. Wouldn't the spotlight be turned onto the political aspects of the case?

The more I thought about it, the more I was overcome with a surge of anxieties: Would there be politically motivated attacks against me? Would my address be leaked? Would it cause trouble for my family and friends as well?

And if any of these things actually happened, how would

I handle it? How would I protect myself as well as the people around me? It had taken me almost two years to be able to start sleeping again, but now the restless nights returned.

My hair started to fall out, most likely from stress. I couldn't bear the sight of my raggedy appearance in the mirror, so I cut my hair.

I had always worn my hair long. I'd had a short hairstyle back in elementary school, but that had been the first and last time. I chopped off about fifteen inches of my hair—now I had a bob. It felt as though I were shearing away the past.

Confronting the undeniable emotional toll of my situation and its physical manifestation was painful for me. The next step I was about to take—going public—would require tremendous fortitude. The ritual of cutting off my hair served as a way of psyching myself up for what was to come. Even if it was an insignificant gesture, I was strangely nervous beforehand. But afterward, I was so unexpectedly calm about the bob I even thought, *Maybe I should shave it all off?* That way, I wouldn't need to worry at all about my hair falling out.

The Interview in *Shukan Shincho*

In the midst of my planning, I was contacted again by Kiyoshi Shimizu. He wanted to know how things were going, so we arranged a meeting to catch up, and when I saw him, he conveyed that the weekly *Shukan Shincho* had proposed reporting on the incident, with himself acting as intermediary. Apparently, they had been following the case since 2016, but had not managed to get in touch with me.

"I'll talk to you about the facts I have on hand and the truth of the matter," I responded. And I told him that, if they wanted to write an objective story, they would need to interview Mr. Yamaguchi as well. There was no way for me to know what kind of angle the resulting article would produce.

Nevertheless, if they wanted to hear what I had to say, then I would do as I had all along—I had made up my mind to tell the same story. I wouldn't run away or hide.

Then, just as the arrangements were being finalized, I had to leave Japan to cover a story in Colombia. I had made contact with the National Liberation Army, the left-wing guerrilla group that had been negotiating with the Colombian government for a peace agreement. My goal was to report on the situation on the ground and to interview a female soldier.

I had been terribly preoccupied with the press conference, so I was thrilled by the opportunity to throw myself into a work project.

While I was in Colombia, I heard from *Shukan Shincho* again. They really wanted to do the story, they said, and wanted to see me when I returned to Japan.

I met with them soon after I got back in May. Mr. Shimizu and the editor in chief both attended the meeting. The editors wanted to get started on the story right away. I agreed to cooperate with their reporting in exchange for their guarantee to explain in the article the main reasons why I decided to speak to them: the necessity for systemic change within investigative practices and the legal system, as well as assault hotlines, and the importance of current efforts within the Diet to amend the law.

I had already resolved to speak on the record, without hiding my face or name, but Mr. Kiyoshi advised me that it was better not to do so at this stage, and the reporters from *Shukan Shincho* agreed with him.

The first article was published in the May 18 issue of *Shukan Shincho*, which went on sale on May 10, less than a week after our meeting.

I very much wanted to discuss the publication with my lawyers, but all this happened around Golden Week, and we weren't able to see each other.

The day after I met with the journalists from *Shukan Shincho*, they started their reporting at the Sheraton Miyako Hotel. The person in charge of security there was former police, so he alerted MPD immediately about reporters contacting the hotel.

What would happen after the article appeared?

There was no way to predict, but seeing as how things were already in motion, the editors decided that it would be dangerous to delay publication.

It turned out they were right.

Based on the events that lead to the case's dismissal, who knew what kind of interference might appear, or where from.

The *Shukan Shincho* reporters had asked me to alert them right away if I noticed anything unusual. They had promised to move me to a secure location if there was any suspicious activity near where I lived. On the day before receiving the proofs for the article, I noticed something, so I packed a bag and left my apartment.

The issue went on sale without incident.

In the article, the content relating to the attack was struc-
tured around the emails, testimony, and evidence that Mr. A.
and I had methodically assembled.

But the bombshell that had been uncovered in their
reporting was an admission from the then chief of Criminal Investigation at MPD: "I was the one who called off Mr.
Yamaguchi's arrest."

"The Final Decision Was Mine"

Here is a summary of the article:

> According to an analysis by our reporters at MPD who
> are familiar with this case, the progress of the investi-
> gation by the Takanawa Police Department was being
> reported to MPD First Investigation Division (Criminal
> Investigation) in the period leading up to the issuance of
> Mr. Yamaguchi's arrest warrant. There was an under-
> standing that, because the matter concerned quasi-rape,
> it would require an arrest by force, rather than a volun-
> tary one.
>
> However, when the head of the Public Information
> Division at MPD got wind of the "Yamaguchi Arrest,"
> he recognized the gravity of arresting a journalist from
> TBS, and he alerted the chief of Criminal Investigation
> and the MPD commissioner.
>
> It was rumored that the person likely to have ordered
> the cover-up was the chief of Criminal Investigation at
> the time, Itaru Nakamura, who had earned immense

trust from Chief Cabinet Secretary Yoshihide Suga, for whom he had served as executive secretary.

Mr. Nakamura was an ace who had entered MPD in 1986. He had served under Mr. Suga when the Democratic Party of Japan was in power, and should have been relieved from his post when the Liberal Democratic Party took back power, but he implored Mr. Suga to keep him on.

By remaining in his post, Mr. Nakamura was able to demonstrate his crisis management skills, which surely did not go unappreciated by Mr. Suga, who saw his potential as a future commissioner-general of the National Police Agency.

When *Shukan Shincho* reporters asked Mr. Nakamura whether suspending the investigation was the expressed will of his superiors, or if he had surmised it to be their will, his answer was: "That's preposterous. This had nothing to do with [Mr. Yamaguchi's social standing]. As for the substance of the case, the final decision was mine [that there was no need to arrest him]. It was a matter of course [that the investigation be suspended]. I recall making the decision myself. Just look at how the case turned out in the end . . ."

Shukan Shincho, May 18, 2017 issue

Mr. Yamaguchi himself responded in an unexpected way to *Shukan Shincho*: when the editors sent him an interview request, he apparently intended to forward the message to someone named Kitamura but inadvertently replied to the *Shukan Shincho* editors. They reported on it in their subsequent issue, a summary of which follows:

184

On May 8, Mr. Yamaguchi posted on his Facebook page his opinion about being interviewed by *Shukan Shincho*, and this post was liked by Akie Abe, the wife of the prime minister. In addition, here is what transpired when we emailed Mr. Yamaguchi an interview request:

For some reason, the editorial department received a response that read, "Dear Mr. Kitamura, this questionnaire arrived from *Shukan Shincho*. It's about Ito."

Having intended to forward the email to "Mr. Kitamura," he had mistakenly replied to us, the editors. The text of the message makes clear that the matter had previously been discussed between Mr. Yamaguchi and Mr. Kitamura, and that they regarded it as a problem.

Hearing the name Kitamura, the person who comes to mind is none other than Shigeru Kitamura, the Director of Cabinet Intelligence.

Mr. Kitamura, who for five years has held the top post in the Cabinet Intelligence and Research Office and who oversees all intelligence both at home and abroad, is expected to take the post of Deputy Chief Cabinet Secretary this summer. This year alone, Mr. Kitamura's name has appeared fifty-four times in the list of Prime Minister Abe's activities, and it is safe to assume that they are also in contact behind the scenes, as Mr. Kitamura is a member of the prime minister's inner circle.

When *Shukan Shincho* inquired with Mr. Yamaguchi, he denied that it was Shigeru Kitamura.

"This person is a private citizen with whom I consult on various matters, including the one in question. It is not the individual you named."

And Mr. Kitamura's response:

"I have no answer for you, my apologies." In response to the question of how long he had been consulted on the matter: "No, that's all. Thank you, goodbye."

When we asked journalists familiar with the relationship between the prime minister's office and Mr. Yamaguchi, the unanimous answer was that it could only be Shigeru Kitamura. The chief of Criminal Investigation at MPD, Akie Abe, Shigeru Kitamura—is it a coincidence that the people surrounding Mr. Yamaguchi all have close ties with the prime minister?

Above all, had the chief of MPD's Criminal Investigation at the time, Itaru Nakamura, not obstructed the investigation of the jurisdictional authority, the Takanawa Police Department, and squashed the arrest warrant, then it would not have been possible for Mr. Yamaguchi to have risen to stardom with the publication of his biography of Shinzo Abe, nor would he have his career as a commentator that followed.

Shukan Shincho, May 25, 2017 issue

The two revelations—that Itaru Nakamura, chief of Criminal Investigation at the time, admitted that it was his own decision to call off the arrest, and that Mr. Yamaguchi had been previously consulting with "Mr. Kitamura" about me—were truly major developments.

My honest reaction is that I never would have expected Mr. Nakamura, in particular, to have made such an admission. The *Shukan Shincho* team had done superb reporting.

After two years of pleading the same case, with no discernible change, this signified tremendous progress.

CHAPTER EIGHT
BEARING WITNESS

The *Shukan Shincho* article triggered major developments in my case. But the article's slant did not necessarily align with my own agenda. Certainly, the link between Mr. Yamaguchi's personal connections and the arrest being called off was essential context for the case. And I'll say it again, I am grateful to the reporters for revealing this with such clarity.

However, the things I was most determined to communicate were the systemic problems within the legal system and investigative process that compelled victims to give up and suffer in silence, as well as society's role in perpetuating these issues. I had agreed to cooperate in the reporting on the condition that my reasons for speaking out were included in the final article.

And yet, my motivations remained widely misunderstood.

Not "Victim A"

In the previous articles, I had remained nameless and faceless, "the female victim." I did not like how this unavoidable label clung to me. Being a victim was not my job, nor was it part of my character. As I prepared to tell the world my story, I despaired at the prospect of having to live with this label for the rest of my life.

In various incidents over recent years, victims' families have come forward, using their real names and photographs, to tell their stories on the news. In 2015, Matsuri Takahashi was driven to suicide due to stress from overwork at the advertising company Dentsu. And in 2016, the middle school student Rima Kasai died by suicide because of being bullied.

After the heartbreak of losing their beloved children, these families demonstrated immense courage in telling their stories to the media, in the hope that such things would not happen again.

It was because these people had appeared with their real names and faces, not just as "Victim A," that their message had had a larger impact. And seeing their example, I made up my mind not to be "Victim A" either. I was determined, again, to hold a press conference.

I hoped that fewer women would have to go through what I did—my experience was an ordeal that I wished upon no one. Rape could no longer be something that "happens all the time."

Mr. A. had told me that the lessons he had learned from my case would be put to use in future cases. When I heard the words "future cases," the faces of people I loved flashed before my eyes. The mere thought of something like this happening to them terrified me. Even this very moment, there are people suffering. With them in mind, I knew if I didn't act now to change the system, I would regret it for the rest of my life.

On the other hand, I was afraid of exposing my wounds to other people. My scars had only just started to heal—wouldn't this rip them open all over again? A press conference would essentially mean publicly revealing those wounds and having strangers pour salt on them.

The friends who had been with me the past two years, always helping me figure out what to do, supported me in this decision. I made plans to tell my family. I had already put my parents through so much heartache, and I felt terrible about causing them any further trouble. I had previously spoken to them about my intention to appear jointly with other sexual assault victims in a press conference calling for revisions to the law. At first, out of worry for me, they had been against the idea, but they had come around to accepting it.

This time, however, they were completely opposed. Up until now, I hadn't told them in detail about the attack— it was only upon reading the articles that they had learned everything that had happened to me, and it must have been extremely painful for them.

My mother said, "Now that the articles are out, everyone knows what happened to you. I don't want you to do a press conference, absolutely not. You already feel unsafe enough that you're staying with K.—why would you expose yourself more? What if photographers suddenly appear out of nowhere?"

Her reaction to me holding a press conference using my real name and face was understandable. I myself had agonized over what I would do if this actually resulted in any harm coming to my family.

My father said, "More than fighting to change society, I

just want you to be a happy person. A parent's only wish for their daughter is that she live a life for herself—to be happily married and to create a loving family."

That was what any parent wanted for their child.

Silence Does Not Bring Peace

Indeed, as my father said, pretending that nothing had happened might not have caused any harm. But that didn't necessarily mean that silence would bring peace. At least, for me, I couldn't be happy if I remained silent.

My mother said, with tears streaming down her face, "Nothing can change what's happened. But, right before the attack, you told me about this person who thought you had potential, that you were going to meet him. Hearing that, why didn't I warn you to be careful with him? Isn't that what a mother is supposed to do?"

It pained me to see her blame herself. I was filled with remorse.

Then my mother gave a little smile. "Your mind is made up, though, isn't it? This is to let us know that you're doing it, not a discussion. That's always been your way."

I feel especially sorry—even now—about my younger sister's feelings. Until the very end, she was against me holding a press conference.

"I understand what you're saying. About how important this is, and that you're doing it for me and my friends. But why does it have to be you?" she pleaded. "I can imagine if the press conference were in English. But don't do it in

Japanese, with only Japanese media there," she added. And then, knowing me so well, she murmured these last words, "But you're going to do it anyway." It's still hard for me that she couldn't understand.

I put so much energy into this press conference because I didn't want her or the people who were dear to me to ever face anything like what had happened to me.

I hope that one day, my sister will understand that.

Not an Easy Press Conference

On May 29, 2017, I held a press conference at the kisha club for judiciary reporters on the second floor of the Tokyo District Court.

Things did not go the way I expected.

Holding a press conference was an opportunity for me to speak directly to the mainstream press who had, up until then, not covered my case at all. As such, I faced resistance at first.

One newspaper journalist said, "If it were my own daughter, I'd never allow her to be bombarded with questions from reporters who, knowing they'd never be able to run the story, had only come out of sheer curiosity."

Although *Shukan Shincho* had published those articles, there had been surprisingly little follow-up coverage elsewhere. I had hoped that there would be a more open discussion about lingering doubts concerning the decisions made by the investigating authorities.

The things that I wanted to call attention to hadn't

changed, but now my petition to the Committee for the Inquest of the Prosecution provided a turning point for holding a press conference. And for that reason, it seemed fitting to speak about it at the kisha club for judiciary reporters at the courthouse. By doing so, if the Japanese media still didn't cover my story, it would discredit the Japanese media system itself.

To reduce whatever pressure there might be, we had decided to announce the press conference the day before it was scheduled to take place.

With the date of the conference a few days away, I spoke with Kiyoshi Shimizu about it. On the call, he said to me, "You've made the right decision."

But that very evening, he called back to say, "No one will run the story if you hold it at the kisha club for judiciary reporters. Don't do it—this will only cause you harm. The only option is to move it to the Foreign Correspondents' Club."

I was in shock.

Until then, Mr. Shimizu had been supportive of the press conference, so hearing this from him shook my resolve.

The following day, I was contacted by another journalist I knew.

"The government is recommending to media outlets that they ought not to cover the story, that the sources are not reliable. As you can imagine, these outlets were already intimidated, so who's to say whether or not anyone will cover the press conference . . ."

He went on, "The press conference should still happen—

it'll just take some ingenuity. What's inexplicable, though, is why the government feels the need to intervene this way."

I felt incredibly confused by these calls, coming in such rapid succession.

When I mentioned to one of the reporters from *Shukan Shincho* that there seemed to be an undercurrent discouraging the media from covering my press conference, the tone of his response—"Yes, I've heard"—was rather light, as if to say, *So what?* I found this quite heartening.

Taking some of Mr. Shimizu's advice, I planned to hold another event at the Foreign Correspondents' Club of Japan (FCCJ) immediately following the press conference at the kisha club for judiciary reporters. This would ensure that not only foreign media but also Japanese media who weren't members of the kisha club would be able to attend. There also weren't the same domestic pressures at FCCJ.

But when I made a formal request to FCCJ, they declined to host my press conference.

"Too personal, too sensitive" was the reason given.

But weren't all experiences personal in some way? FCCJ had previously hosted press conferences for victims of sexual assault and stalkers. I couldn't help but wonder who thought my story was "too sensitive"?

I had never heard of any other instances of FCCJ not allowing a press conference.

After noticing suspicious activity near my apartment, I had gone to stay at my friend K.'s place, but I had only brought a few things with me—just T-shirts and jeans. I hadn't intended to appear at the press conference in a brand new outfit, but I couldn't very well wear jeans and a T-shirt to the courthouse. When I ventured to the shopping district to buy some suitable clothes, I had a panic attack.

After I'd held the press conference, would people on the street only see me as a "rape victim"? The mere thought of it terrified me.

Don't Shut Down

Once I decided to hold the press conference, I started running.

At first it could barely be called running. I mean, it had been more than ten years since I'd played sports. At one point in my past, when my father nearly died and I was having doubts about a relationship I had gotten myself into, I had gone on a yoga retreat in India. I ended up devoting myself to the practice and getting certified as a yoga instructor. I had thought that my day-to-day work with camera equipment would have helped me maintain a strong physique, but I had mistaken fatigue for the exhaustion that comes from physical labor. I wasn't as strong I used to be.

On May 29, the day of the press conference, I rose early to go for a run. Later, K. told me that she had been quite worried when she woke up and I wasn't there.

Despite all my anxiety leading up to the event, I felt I handled myself pretty well at the press conference. But I mentioned that the Diet had been drawing out deliberations on an anti-conspiracy law, which delayed their discussion about revisions to the criminal law on rape. My remarks were misconstrued as overtly political—I was surprised by the way that the internet went wild with speculation that I must have been a plant for the Democratic Party.

I experienced firsthand the way that "fake news" is manufactured.

Following the press conference, my personal information was made public. I was harassed and threatened, and I was bombarded with scathing emails.

My mother told me not to contact my sister. She was very hurt by what I'd done. As my mother said, my sister had always been proud of me as her big sister—even all her friends liked me.

At the time of writing this book, my sister and I still hadn't spoken since the press conference. Being younger, her generation has had access to many more things on the internet—surely plenty of things they would have rather not seen. The thought of this still pains me.

My cell phone rang constantly. For a while, K. held on to it, answering calls for me. At one point, I couldn't even set foot outside, and I am grateful to K. for supporting me in ways that my family wasn't able to at the time.

I must have been even more tense about the press conference than I realized, because once it was over, the fatigue rushed in.

Immediately following the press conference, as I was fielding numerous requests for interviews on the way home, I collapsed. Luckily a friend was with me at the time, and she took me straight to the hospital.

I was bedridden for days. I didn't have the strength to chew, though I had no appetite anyway. I didn't eat solid food for more than a week. I couldn't breathe deeply, and my body felt cold to the touch, like a corpse.

All I wanted was to shut everything out and for it to be over.

Ten days after the press conference, I was finally able to take in a bit of food, and little by little, I started eating again. I regained some strength.

This was not the moment to shut down. The victim, facing a bashing after giving a press conference, has a complete breakdown—that was the exact scenario I had hoped to avoid. I wanted to enable an open conversation about sexual violence in Japanese society. It wouldn't do to fall silent now.

I kept on running.

While I was staying at K.'s house, still unable to go outside following the press conference, K.'s fiancé started teaching me kickboxing. He kindly pointed out that he ought to have started these lessons sooner, but the training was merciless anyway.

He barked at me like a tough drill sergeant, and though at first I was so scared I had to squeeze my eyes shut, I strapped on gloves and practiced punches and defense. Still afraid to go outside, I was grateful for the ability to exercise inside the house.

One time, I took a blow to my side body in a surprise move. I got angry with myself for being lulled into a sense of security with K.'s fiancé, and for losing my concentration.

Staggering from the pain, I felt my fighting spirit switch back on for the first time in a long while.

No Matter Who I Am,
It Does Not Change the Facts

K.'s fiancé loved martial arts, and I started watching UFC— Ultimate Fighting Championship—matches with him. That's where I first saw Ronda Rousey, the inaugural UFC Women's Bantamweight Champion, who KO'ed her opponent with a single kick.

She had quite an impact on me.

I became fascinated by images of Ronda, by how committed she was to her training. From then on, I thought of her during my own practice, hoping to become even a little bit like her.

When I first started running, I could barely run over a mile, but gradually I was able to increase my distance. Now I run close to six miles a day. I couldn't help but enjoy seeing my body respond to the exercise, and develop endurance and stamina.

When it was too hot to run during the daytime, I would run at night. I was still filled with anxiety, but since I had started sparring, my fear had lessened.

Exercise worked wonders for my mental stability, more than any medicine ever could have.

Here's something I became acutely aware of after the press conference: Why is it that people are always so focused on what there is to gain from doing something?

Just look at how the press conference was criticized. People said, "She wouldn't have done that unless it was for something in it for her." Meaning it must have been a publicity stunt or a honey trap, or that my actions were politically motivated.

Out of respect for my family, I had not revealed my last name at the press conference, and this decision was also scrutinized, with people speculating that I was a Zainichi Korean.

What was all this about? And if any of it were true, what difference did it make?

I'm not a left-wing activist, both of my parents are Japanese, and I'm a Japanese citizen. But even if I were left-wing or a Democratic Party Diet member or of Korean nationality, none of these things would make it acceptable for me to be the target of sexual violence. Nor should it make me the target of criticism or blame. No matter who I am, it does not change the facts of what happened to me.

Determined to Believe

By going public about the assault, I knew that I needed to be prepared for the fact that I would no longer be able to work for a Japanese company—or even work in Japan at all. I'd been told from the start, "If you file a complaint, it will make it difficult for you to find work in the journalism world," and had heard those words repeated countless times over the course of the investigation.

Perhaps this was understandable, seeing as how I was

speaking out against the Washington bureau chief of TBS who had deep political ties. But just how would I have gotten by in Japan's male-dominated news industry anyway?

Although my desire to do truth-seeking work was unwavering, I also wondered how I would manage to find employment outside of Japan when all I had was a Japanese passport. I still had very little experience—would that really be enough for me to get a permit to work abroad?

It seemed hard to imagine.

I had no choice but to believe in my own abilities. To believe that I was capable of continuing to work, even if I could no longer do so within the media organizations in Japan.

These past two years, I had learned that there were many ways of making a living. In case I was going to be completely shut out in Japan, I started reaching out to foreign media companies. I still had the idea for a documentary on elderly people dying alone that I hadn't been able to squeeze into three minutes, along with some other ideas. The first place I brought them to was BBC's headquarters in London.

I was so nervous when I gave my name to the person who commissions international documentaries for BBC London, but once I started discussing my ideas, my apprehension vanished, and I poured all my energy into conveying how important these subjects were to me.

I kept knocking on doors, reaching out to whatever media organizations I came across. Talks moved forward, and just as my first project was being finalized with BBC, the media company Channel News Asia (CNA), based in Singapore, expressed interest in producing the project as a one-hour program. In the end, rather than use BBC's twenty-four-minute format, I decided to work with CNA, whose longer format would allow me to report on the story in more depth.

In the meantime, one-off projects and documentary production gigs had also started to trickle in.

Looking back on that period, I'm so glad that I chose to believe in myself, instead of simply accepting that I wouldn't be able to keep working in the media and that all the hard work I'd done would "go to waste." I enjoyed the balance between documentary work that required time and research, and shorter one-off projects. I never would have been able to do this kind of reporting while working for a typical news agency.

And even if I didn't like the fact that my speaking out against the legal system and investigative process had been criticized as a publicity stunt, perhaps I ought to take comfort—at the very least, it offered proof that I had succeeded in raising awareness of these issues.

Ruled by Fear, without Even Realizing It

Two months after the press conference, in the summer of 2017, my parents insisted upon taking me to see a psychiatrist.

I had seen a counselor during the investigation who had diagnosed me with PTSD. But I saw therapy as nothing more than the painful task of revisiting memories I'd rather forget in order to get a prescription for medication. I hated the idea of having to recount my suffering all over again.

What's more, I had just been invited to London by an English human rights group and was already preparing to leave Japan.

From my parents' perspective, I was in a dangerous condition, stricken with symptoms of depression and sudden suicidal thoughts ever since the press conference. It goes without saying that they were opposed to me going to England "in such a mental state."

But I had been dealing with these symptoms for two years; they hadn't just suddenly appeared. After the press conference, it had been particularly difficult for me to lead a normal life. During that acutely painful period, when I was unable to leave the house freely, I needed support and all I wanted was a place where I could go to take my mind off things.

But no matter how many times I explained this to them, my parents remained convinced that the only thing that would save me was seeing a psychiatrist. Or rather, that was the only solution they could come up with.

With no other way to appease them, I met with a doctor a few days before my departure.

This time, I decided I would be clear about what exactly it was that I needed. Specifically, what I should do when I experienced a panic attack brought on by PTSD.

The doctor acknowledged the effects I had seen from exercise, pointing out the benefits of elevating my heart rate by running. But, he said, although PTSD was not something that could be cured by taking medicine, there were effective treatments. He told me about a method called eye movement desensitization and reprocessing (EMDR).

A form of therapy in which treatment is administered in the form of rapid eye movement, EMDR has similarities with hypnosis using a pendant on a string. It was originally developed to treat soldiers who were suffering PTSD after returning from war.

Because I was about to go abroad, the doctor simply told me that this treatment existed—and left it at that.

Since I haven't personally tried EMDR, I can't attest to its effectiveness, but there is an episode of the Netflix show *Black Mirror* that made me think about it.

Black Mirror is a science fiction anthology series in which technology is slightly more advanced than present day, or has gone too far, and each episode examines the effects it can have on people's daily lives.

In this particular episode, a troop of soldiers have been sent to kill humanoid mutants called "roaches" who are carrying a terrible infectious disease. Only later does one of the soldiers realize that the army has programmed them to view these ordinary human beings as roaches to make them easier to kill.

The soldier who learns that he has murdered people who have real names and faces is disturbed by what he has done. He visits an army psychologist who says that he can erase his memories that the roaches are actually humans, but to do so, the soldier must give his consent. *What should he do?* he wonders.

When I saw this, I couldn't help but be reminded of EMDR.

It goes without saying that reducing my PTSD attacks

was exactly what I wanted, but how could it be that eye movements could lessen my suffering? When I inquired with a psychiatrist in England about it, he confirmed that the treatment allowed you to control your emotions. But by using this particular method to reduce suffering, doesn't it also diminish the sense of danger that one feels toward this problem they've been struggling with all this time?

I didn't know what to think anymore.

It then occurred to me that, without even realizing it, ever since being violently sexually assaulted against my will, I had been ruled by fear. The memory loss deeply frightened me. I thought I had control over my own body, but someone else had been able to take over.

That explained why, just after the attack, I had felt like an empty shell, like I'd been destroyed.

"Before, you seemed like a strong, capable woman, but now you're like a troubled child. It's adorable."

That was what Mr. Yamaguchi had said to me when I had told him to give back my underwear that he had asked to keep "as a souvenir." My knees had given out under me, and I had collapsed in a heap.

The essence of what he said would seem to reveal his desire to dominate, to subjugate. Several months before the press conference, what I had learned in my reporting on chikan (public groping) was that it went beyond a sexual predilection, this desire for domination and subjugation.

For the perpetrator, it takes no more than a moment to satisfy his desire. But for the person on the other end of the experience, it will mark them for life.

The Bathing Suit I Only Wore Once

When I was young, I had numerous experiences of chikan.

The first time was at the library. I must have been in second grade or so. My father had brought my younger brother and me to the library, and I was sitting on a bench, reading a book, when a middle-aged man looked up my skirt.

There was something very unnatural about what he had done, and scary, but because it confused me, I didn't tell anyone about it.

The next time I remember it happening was two years later, when I was riding the train by myself. The car wasn't very crowded, and a man came up behind me. At first I didn't understand the need for him to stand so close to me, but in an instant, as I was gripping the hand strap, my entire body went rigid. The man pressed against me, touching my body over my clothes. It must have been ten or fifteen minutes until we reached the station where I got off the train. I was paralyzed with fear, but I remember sprinting out of the train car and toward the ticket gate, hoping he wasn't following me.

It was perfectly clear to me that there was something strange about this, that there was something wrong with that man, but at the time I still had no idea what it was that had been done to me.

"There was a strange man on the train today" was the extent of what I could say to my mother about it. To this day, I can still recall facing the train window with the afternoon sun shining through it, and as I held on to the strap, the sight of the flickering reflection of my rigid body against the landscape as it went by. I remember the pale blue and orange jacket I was wearing, but I couldn't see the man's face. I never turned around.

The third time, I was in my last year of elementary school—I must have been eleven years old. My family went to a water park called Tokyo Summerland with my friend and her family. We had been planning for and looking forward to this trip for a long time, and the day finally arrived. I had just started reading magazines for kids, and had pestered my mother to buy me my first bikini, one I had seen in those pages.

I had always loved swimming, and up until the moment when this happened, I had hoped the day would never end.

What spoiled everything was a man's selfish act. It was a weekend, or maybe summer vacation, and the wave pool was filled with people, jostling up against each other. I was in a large float ring, and my friend and I swam out toward the waves. At one point, my feet no longer could touch the bottom. But it didn't matter how deep it was—I wasn't scared of the water at all. I just kept heading for the waves.

My friend had slipped her way in between the other swimmers and was now far out in front of me. There were so many people and, trying not to lose sight of her, I called out, "Wait for me!"

Just at that moment, a hand suddenly grabbed me from behind in the water. Touching my body, specifically the part of me covered by my bikini. Since my feet didn't reach the bottom, I had to hold on to my float ring with both arms, my legs dangling beneath. The rest of me was hidden by the float ring, so the people around me probably couldn't see.

I don't know how long it went on for—I was again paralyzed with fear. My eyes searched desperately for my friend, I called out her name, I tried to scream "Help!" but almost no sound came out. There were so many people around me, but even if I had been able to call out, would anyone have rescued me?

And yet, no matter how I tried to scream, it was like my voice had been wrung out—I barely made any sound in that noisy pool filled with shrieking children.

It may have only lasted a minute, but it felt like forever. Finally, my friend noticed that I wasn't anywhere near her and she turned to look in my direction. She headed back toward me, a huge smile on her face, and all the while, the hands that reached out from behind me never stopped moving.

When she was about ten feet away from me, I was released from the torture at last. I must have looked totally scared and confused. My friend immediately asked, "What's wrong?"

All I said was "Somebody touched me," and I turned around to look behind me.

I saw a slender man moving away from us.

"Did you see that guy behind me just now?" I asked.

"Yeah, a young guy," my friend replied.

I couldn't keep swimming and having fun. I was too scared. Even at the age of eleven, I still didn't understand the situation—all I felt was confusion. And I can still vividly recall the tremendous fear and sense of revulsion that came over me.

We hurried back to where our families were waiting, spread out on a blue vinyl sheet.

"A man touched me."

I didn't know how to talk about it, so that was all I said. My mother put a towel around me and told me to rest.

Feeling safe at last, tears came to my eyes. But I didn't want the other family or my friend, who were still enjoying themselves, to notice, so I just sat there quietly, wrapped in my towel.

"It's because you're wearing such a cute bikini."

My friend's mother may have been trying to make me feel better, but her words shattered me. She implied that it had been my fault. Did I really need to worry about what I wore? I was the one being blamed just for wearing the bathing suit that I had wanted so badly, and this made me very sad.

I never wore that bathing suit again.

There's No Such Thing as "Clothing a Victim Wears"

I bring up these experiences because I want to show how there's no connection between what a person is wearing and the likelihood of being assaulted. For the press conference, when the journalist Kiyoshi Shimizu, in whom I have the utmost trust, told me to wear a dark "recruitment" suit, like for a corporate interview, I categorically refused on the spot.

As I previously mentioned, knowing that jeans and a T-shirt simply wouldn't do, I decided to wear a linen shirt. Of course, Mr. Shimizu knows the Japanese media very well, and I'm very grateful for the support he gave me. It's just that I wanted to do away with the preconceived image of a victim wearing a white shirt, buttoned all the way up, looking sad.

No one should be blamed for what they choose to wear or not to wear, and it should never be used as an excuse for why an assault occurred.

I refuse to be confined to the stereotype of a victim, which I believe is flawed to begin with.

Groping is a criminal act that occurs even on the train to or from school. The last time I was the victim of chikan, I was wearing my school uniform. I did everything I could to avoid the middle-aged man on the train, moving around and changing places, but he kept following me. Seeing the pleased look on his face as he observed my discomfort filled me with rage.

I had learned from past experiences and decided that, the next time it happened, I would confront the man. Before I had been too young and, paired with the shock from an inability to understand what I was being put through, no one had ever taught me that this was a "bad thing."

Yet, when it happened again, I tried to raise my voice but nothing came out. And I was afraid that, if I grabbed his hand, he would hit me. We were on an express train, and although my stop was next, it seemed to take forever to get there. The man paid no attention, he kept touching me.

When we finally reached the station, the moment the doors opened I leaped onto the platform and turned back toward the train.

"This man's a pervert! You're a dirty old man, asshole!" I screamed, and then I ran like hell for home, in tears. I must have been fourteen or fifteen years old. This was the first time in my life that I cursed at a total stranger. I had channeled all those terrifying experiences, all of my pent-up frustration and powerlessness, into calling that dirty old man an asshole.

I vowed that the next time someone touched me, I would grab him and turn him over to the police. That vigilance must have shown on my face, because after that, I never had any more experiences with chikan.

We ought to live in a society where we can go about our daily lives without these concerns or the need to make such resolutions. But from my friends' experiences alone, I know that chikan still takes place every day.

A hand slipped into your underwear, your skirt cut open, semen ejaculated on you, being pushed down on the way home from school and your underwear removed, a high school girl surrounded by five or six middle school boys on the train and groped.

All of these attacks happened to friends of mine. And the list could go on and on.

I have a childhood friend who has been the target of chikan quite often, and together we tried to come up with strategies for decreasing these attacks. One that seemed to work was changing her walking style. My friend had a habit of strolling, with a pigeon-toe gait. She trained herself to take long strides and to walk more quickly.

From what I know, perpetrators of chikan often seek out "nice" girls who seem unlikely to challenge the groping, quiet girls, or girls who still don't understand what is being done to them.

I saw these survey results on *Asa-ichi*, a morning show on NHK (the Japan Broadcasting Corporation):

"Things That Lead You to Think That the Other Person Consents to Sex":
— Eating together, just the two of you   11%
— Drinking together, just the two of you   27%
— Getting in a car, just the two of you   25%
— Revealing clothes   23%
— Being drunk   35%

There's not a single item in this list that indicates sexual consent.

Seeing this survey reminded me of a quote from Itaru Nakamura in the article that appeared in *Shukan Shincho*'s May 25, 2017, issue: "She wanted him to help her find a job, and this expectation is why she went out drinking with him, so it's a male-female dispute, after all. And she did go along with him to a second restaurant."

I couldn't believe the former chief of Criminal Investigation at MPD said these words.

If the items from the NHK survey could all be construed as indicating sexual consent, it would mean that women could no longer have a meal with a man, just the two of them. At Japanese corporations, in particular, going out to eat with business acquaintances is very common. Sometimes it's even compulsory.

In my situation, I hadn't planned on having dinner with Mr. Yamaguchi, just the two of us, but that's how things ended up, and we needed to talk about business and hiring prospects.

That day, why didn't I go straight to the police from the hotel?

I've blamed myself so many times for that. A part of me

thought that I would be able to work it out on my own, for myself. Or that it had all been a bad dream.

Still, it's even more painful to hear people who know nothing about the circumstances ask me why I didn't go straight to the police—it feels as though I'm being strangled.

First and foremost, all I could think about was getting to a safe place. Then I wanted to figure out what condition I was in, what the situation was. Why did I have no memory of going to the hotel? And what had happened was extremely humiliating. The word "embarrassing" does not even begin to describe the experience.

But above all, I had trusted Mr. Yamaguchi. I had thought he was going to be my boss. I had a sense of respect for him, as the Washington bureau chief of TBS. How could I suddenly see him as a predator?

And yet, I knew in my heart that what had happened was a criminal act. That it had been terribly violent, and that this act had inflicted grave injury to my spirit.

These two conflicting sentiments confounded me for quite some time.

No Surge of Anger

When I say that I don't feel any anger or hatred toward Mr. Yamaguchi, I get all sorts of heated responses. People tell me that if I say this publicly, no one will think I want to fight a legal battle, that my case will be deemed as lacking criminality, that it's not in my best interest.

Of course, I wanted Mr. Yamaguchi to receive a fair and impartial trial in Japan's judiciary system.

But I couldn't lie about how I felt. The truth was, when I searched my heart, I found nothing resembling anger.

It may be that this was merely one way of protecting myself. Regardless, plenty of people around me shouldered the burden of anger.

When I was exchanging emails with Mr. Yamaguchi, even maintaining an electronic connection with him was unbearable, so like I mentioned before, my friends helped me draft the messages. The emails they composed were filled with outrage, and each time I had to go back through and rewrite them. I consider myself lucky to be surrounded by friends who are so angry on my behalf.

It took one year and four months from the assault to the case's dismissal. After the decision was announced, another ten months were needed to submit for discovery and information gathering, to conduct my own investigation, and to prepare written statements for the Committee for the Inquest of the Prosecution. Had the arrest warrant been executed, it would have been several months before the results were announced.

Unless we call out things that we see as abnormal, we have no choice but to accept the wanton fate that befalls us. If we remain silent, whatever problems we face will continue to be reflected, like a mirror, for the rest of our own lives as well as the lives of generations to come.

This is why I insist that we consider these matters on such an individual level. Ultimately, the media and corporations and society are made up of individual souls.

These past two years, the media let me down countless times—but in the end I held my own press conference, and by doing so I was able to make my voice heard.

Right after the press conference, I received numerous emails saying, "The same thing happened to me."

In these messages, women described similar attacks that occurred at the company where they worked, or with someone in the same industry. And for almost all of them, this was the first time they were telling anyone about these horrifying experiences. The amount of pain and suffering these women have lived with, having sealed what happened deep inside their hearts—it's suffocating just to imagine it.

Reading these emails—"I've never spoken to anyone about this"—I became even more convinced that holding the press conference was the right thing to do, despite how much it took out of me.

Questions I Have for Itaru Nakamura

Even now, there are two things I would still like to know.

First: Why did you call off the arrest? I would very much like to ask Itaru Nakamura about the basis for his decision. I posed this question repeatedly to MPD's First Investigation Division, and I won't be satisfied until I get the truth, not some bogus excuse.

In preparation for writing this book, I attempted to interview Mr. Nakamura twice, to no avail. I approached him on his way to work and when I called out to him, "I'd like to speak with you," he hurriedly rushed off. Never in my life did I think I'd be chasing after the police.

I simply want an answer. I'd just like for Mr. Nakamura to clearly explain to me the reasoning behind his decision. Why wouldn't the former chief of MPD's Criminal Investigation be able to justify himself? Why would he simply run away from the question?

After the press conference, I learned something from one of the journalists I met. I had been worried about the media prying into my personal life, discovering my address and that of my parents, even meddling with my friends' privacy. The journalist told me, "Answer as many questions as possible, take as many interviews with the weeklies as you can." Avoiding the press makes them think you have a secret, something to hide, he said, and they chase you even more persistently. I heeded his advice in my response to the media, and none of my worst fears came to pass.

As of this writing, I've sent my questions to Mr. Nakamura, and I await his reply. It's unfortunate not to be able to include those in this book, but I look forward to his direct answers in due course.

The other thing I would like to know concerns the investigation report that was compiled after my case was transferred from Takanawa Police Department to MPD's First Investigation Division. The Takanawa Police Department's report on the taxi driver included numerous mentions of my asking him to take me to a train station, so why was this information left out of MPD's report?

After the Committee for the Inquest of the Prosecution's

announced its determination on September 22, 2017, that my case was nonprosecutable, I heard from several journalists about rumors that were circulating: "I saw the security video, but she was walking normally. The taxi driver testified that she cleaned up the vomit herself. Which means that she must have been conscious the whole time, right?" According to one newspaper reporter, these were the reasons why the case had been dismissed.

These are nothing more than rumors, of course, but there's no doubt that someone started them. So then, where did these rumors come from?

This kind of gossip only leads to more questions about the contents of MPD's investigation report.

In conclusion, I will restate the facts.

The following are the objective facts about what happened that night, either confirmed by Mr. Yamaguchi or clarified in the investigation and testimony:

— Noriyuki Yamaguchi, TBS Washington bureau chief, and I, freelance journalist, met to discuss the visa I needed in order to work in TBS's Washington bureau.
— We were not romantically involved.
— Mr. Yamaguchi was aware that I was in a drunken "stupor."
— Mr. Yamaguchi brought me to his hotel room.
— Sexual intercourse occurred.
— The results of a DNA test performed on my bra detected biological material matching Mr. Yamaguchi's Y chromosomes.

— After gathering evidence from the hotel security camera footage and the taxi driver's testimony, the police requested an arrest warrant, which was granted and issued by the court.

— On the day of the arrest, while investigators were on site awaiting Mr. Yamaguchi's arrival at the airport, the execution of the arrest warrant was suddenly called off, in accordance with the decision of Itaru Nakamura, chief of MPD's Criminal Investigation.

The public prosecutor and the Committee for the Inquest of the Prosecution, with knowledge of these facts, decided to dismiss the case as "nonprosecutable."

So, what do you think?

EPILOGUE

More than five years have passed since I experienced instantaneous destruction. And it's been more than three years since this book came out in Japan. Nonstop years these have been.

And in these years, how many times have I appeared in a courtroom? How many times have I spoken publicly about my trauma? How many times have I wished it were all over?

A year after the incident, I was shocked to hear a close friend tell me, "You never laugh the way you used to." I had thought that nothing about me had changed, but the truth is, I am no longer the buoyant and cheerful person I used to be. I was like a balloon that had been punctured but then patched up with duct tape—I didn't have the same bounce.

And yet, I am still me—that hasn't changed.

To be honest, I never wanted anyone to know about what happened to me. I didn't want to think about it or remember it. I didn't want to utter a single word about it.

And frankly, I hated the idea of writing a book. But I made up my mind that, one day, I would tell this story in my own words—either as a book or a documentary.

I thought that, perhaps after ten or twenty years of therapy, the wounds in my heart might not be quite so raw, and I'd be able to find a way to confront what had happened.

While I don't think that time will simply heal everything, I know that I must take the time I need to move forward. Without pushing myself too hard.

Rape is a soul-killing experience. And yet, we go on living, and as the soul gradually heals, we also gradually recover our very selves. Humans are resilient, and there are various ways to heal. For me, the way forward is to seek out the truth, and to make it known to as many people as possible.

No matter how much we wish it otherwise, none of us can return to being the person we were in the past. But the fact is that now, I have no desire to go back to who I was before the rape. From the moment I regained consciousness, I believed in myself and I believed in the truth, and each day that I have lived since then has become an integral part of me.

The suffering I experienced was previously unimaginable to me, and what I know now is that this same suffering is shared by an unfathomable number of people around the world. I hope that this same experience never happens to you, or for you to have to see this happen to someone you love.

And yet, there are so many people whom I would have never had the chance to meet had this not happened to me.

In this way, I have been able to make the most of my experiences. I've had the support of so many dear friends. They've cried with me, drank with me, enjoyed meals with me, run with me, gone on hikes with me. And amid this desperate effort to survive, each day I've managed to smile a little bit more. I'm able to relax more often too. I have fewer sleepless nights. The hard feelings within my family have gradually softened. When my sister calls me on the phone, her voice is light again. "Hey, sis!" she says.

Back when the deadline for this manuscript was fast approaching, I had the opportunity to speak on the phone with Gary Noling, who had written to me about his daughter, Carri Leigh Goodwin. Gary now gives lectures about what happened to her, in the hope of raising awareness about military sexual trauma. To his great sorrow, he learned that Carri's alleged rapist had been accused of another rape two years earlier, but that he was not charged and was able to continue serving in the Marines.

"Maybe if my daughter's rapist had been competently prosecuted in a court of law the first time, she would still be here now," Gary said.

His words illustrate why it is so necessary for the justice system to function properly within society.

Then Gary told me this: "It took an unimaginable amount of courage to do what you did, to go public about what happened to you. It gives us all strength to see the way that you are now fighting for what's right. Surely the path that lies before you will not be easy or smooth, but you must never give up."

Hearing his words, I felt all of the emotions I had been holding in check burst forth, and my tears flowed uncontrollably. That day, I resolved to do my best to convey the determination that I saw reflected in the photograph of Carri.

It is my sincere hope that this book will help to realize that goal, in some small way.

The publication of *Black Box* in Japan coincided with worldwide media coverage of #MeToo in the wake of allegations of sexual abuse and sexual harassment against the Hollywood mega-producer Harvey Weinstein. But even as #MeToo transformed into an undeniable movement in the West, the same voices being raised in Japan were significantly fewer. "In Japan, it's dangerous even to whisper 'me too,'" I heard a lawyer say. This was true. Having been smeared and slandered after I came forward, and having moved to London as a result of the threats I received, I can say with certainty that the internet is not a safe place.

Perhaps the effort to raise our voices in Japan alongside the global #MeToo movement was akin to sticking our heads into a beehive. In Japan there was too much of a lack of understanding about sexual violence and sexual harassment, as well as deeply rooted prejudices and biases against victims. And it's possible that people may have felt that this hit too close to home, that they recognized themselves as both the perpetrators and the perpetrated. I too may have made remarks in the past without realizing that they could have been construed as sexual harassment. Within a society such as Japan, the hurdles involved in joining #MeToo were just too high. And even for those who did speak out, what kinds of support were available? Most people kept quiet, out of fear of secondary victimization amid such a lack of support. Here in Japan, we adapted the hashtag to #WeToo in an effort to overcome that anxiety and to demonstrate that, as members of society, these problems concern all of us. This is based on the attitude that we cannot be passive bystanders, that we cannot tolerate any harassment or sexual violence.

I grew up being told, "You must listen to what grown-ups say."

That was how I was raised. "Be polite to your elders. Don't behave rudely." For those of us who were taught these lessons, how are we supposed to learn to speak up for ourselves?

After being told by the police, "There's nothing we can do," there were plenty of things I managed to accomplish. And yet, the outcome was still that my case was not prosecuted.

People do not want change. In particular, there are people in Japan who still consider it taboo to speak openly about rape.

To them, I ask, what are you trying to protect, and from whom?

In September 2020, I was named one of *Time* magazine's 100 Most Influential People of the Year. "Shiori Ito has forever changed life for Japanese women," the article read. I wonder if that's really true. I understood perhaps for the first time that we must continue this progress, this forward momentum, together.

Since speaking out, I've had many labels attached to my name: victim, Me Too'er, liar, sexual opportunist. And other names—abusive and unprintable words—as well that are still launched at me one after another, like arrows that go straight into my still-healing wounds. Most of these arrows are loosed on the internet, by people whose faces I cannot see. I don't know where they come from. It's frightening to think that the people who aim such hatred toward me are here in Japan, that I might encounter them at some point.

Being on *Time*'s list dispelled all those other labels. It made me feel that I could go on living my life as Shiori Ito. I no longer had to worry or care about being dehumanized or being told that "victims don't smile." It gave me—and us all—the push to say that I could go forth with my head held high. That I could be myself. My mother told me that it made her happy that day to see my smiling face splashed all over the media, for a change.

Every day since the assault has felt like being in the middle of a typhoon. Whenever I think I can relax, I find that it was only the eye of the storm, and in fact everything then swirls and rages around me anew.

Even now this is true. After the *Time* news, another headline appeared about me, concerning the police submitting their report to the public prosecutor's office. I had been sued for defamation and making false accusations.

I received questions from the media along with printouts of all of Mr. Yamaguchi's social media posts. Seeing his words, and the spin he put on things, sent me into a panic. For the first time in a long while, I was overcome with the painful feeling of being unable to breathe. I hate that my body has such a clear memory of the trauma. But this is my daily reality, that I can still easily be thrown into such turmoil.

The police questioned me in a rented conference room, with a view of the beautiful Tokyo sky through the windows. In an attempt to direct my awareness outward, I gazed out

the window of the sterile room. I could see wispy cumulo-
nimbus clouds that seemed to represent the thin line between
summer and fall.

There were four members of MPD present, including
the superintendent.

"What do you think of the accusations?"

I refrained from saying that I was surprised they were
even asking what I thought.

"I'm grateful that this is finally being investigated, but
why is it that this case was accepted?" I turned the question
back around to them.

One of the investigators replied, "Unless there are extraordinary circumstances, when a report is filed we are required
to conduct an investigation if we were not present at the
scene."

Under the 2017 amendment to Japan's criminal law, the
crime of rape was changed to "forced sexual intercourse,"
and the victim is no longer required to file a complaint in
order for the crime to be prosecuted. Although this should
have meant that it would be easier to make a report, I had
received messages from a female university student saying
that she had been turned away when she went to the police
to file a complaint.

And I had been told that the reason my criminal
complaint had not been accepted was "in order to protect
me from injury." Some say that nothing can be done under
the current Japanese criminal code.

In December 2019, the decision in my two-year-long civil
trial for quasi-rape was announced. I won the case, and the
decision acknowledged that "there had not been consent."

If, as in many Western countries, sexual intercourse without consent was routinely prohibited in criminal law, and had I found redress, then perhaps I wouldn't have gone to the length of writing this book.

There are a great many issues that still need to change.

Mr. Yamaguchi's 130-million-yen countersuit for damages—including those incurred by the publication of this book—was dismissed. The alleged damages were deemed "sufficiently public in nature," in relation to the legal and societal reforms that are being called for within these pages.

"You cannot solve a problem that you can't see."

These are the words of Jodi Kantor, the *New York Times* journalist whose investigative reporting on Harvey Weinstein helped ignite the #MeToo movement in 2017.

We have gone from the invisible, nameless existence as victims to "Me."

In my ongoing work to represent the truth, I want to continue to make things visible, to bring them into the light. Because that's how they will change.

Shiori
March 2021

SHIORI ITO is a freelance journalist who contributes news footage and documentaries to the *Economist*, *Al Jazeera*, Reuters, and other primarily non-Japanese media outlets. She was named one of *Time* magazine's 100 Most Influential People of 2020.

ALLISON MARKIN POWELL has been awarded grants from English PEN and the NEA, and the 2020 PEN Translation Prize for *The Ten Loves of Nishino* by Hiromi Kawakami. She is based in New York.

The Feminist Press publishes books that ignite movements and social transformation. Celebrating our legacy, we lift up insurgent and marginalized voices from around the world to build a more just future.

See our complete list of books at
feministpress.org

THE FEMINIST PRESS
AT THE CITY UNIVERSITY OF NEW YORK
FEMINISTPRESS.ORG